To Mark

Thank you for
your support

[signature]

12 GOLDEN KEYS TO HOSPITALITY EXCELLENCE

F. H. Benzakour

12 GOLDEN KEYS TO HOSPITALITY EXCELENCE

Twelve inspiring strategies that can revise a dying country club into a "pièce de résistance" of hospitality excellence.

In the *12 Golden Keys to Hospitality Excellence*, author F. H. Benzakour, Cornell graduate and Professor of Contemporary Club Management at Fairleigh Dickinson University, with twenty-five years of COO experience in taking private clubs from black to green, shares his insights and expertise on superior management.

The twelve strategic, eye-opening approaches, include:

- Over-Invest In People—It's an investment you're guaranteed to reap rewards from.
- Celebrate Diversity—with people of diverse ethnicity and cultures, both members and employees.
- Be A Student of the Obvious—Instead of searching for complex resolutions, look for simple solutions to complicated problems.
- Be A Master of Game Theory—Work out a winning business strategy that will result in a generous payoff
- Swim In Blue Oceans—Create new demand in competition-free market spaces
- The Pareto Principle—Focus on the 20 percent of actions that generate the greatest results
- Innovate or Die—Move toward the future or you'll become part of the past

By employing these twelve dynamic game plans within the *12 Golden Keys to Hospitality Excellence*, managers will advance to being winners in the hospitality industry.

I would like to dedicate this book to my friends and family and to all the special persons who have been part of my life.

With special gratitude to my wife and children for their unconditional love and support during good and "not so good" times. I am aware that I drive them "crazy" with my never-ending projects and I truly appreciate their support. I love you guys more than words can describe, and I truly appreciate and value your commitment to help me become a better person every day.

Introduction and A Little About Me

First, let me set the stage with why I found this to be an opportune time to write this book. The hospitality industry, especially private clubs, are in a time of tremendous transition as they face immense challenges to the traditional way of doing things. The entire industry has had a slowdown. Since the 1940s, the chief lure of country clubs was their magnificent golf courses and the game of golf. However, all over the country, golf is dwindling. Many people who are younger than thirty-five don't play golf, and those people who do golf are playing fewer rounds. In 2016, there were more than 200 golf course closures, and in 2017, five of the finest ocean holes on the eastern seaboard closed. In the US, in 2017, only seventeen new golf courses were built, though there were twenty course expansions. People who enjoy outdoor leisure activities and sports have more options than golf and they don't cost thousands of dollars in initiation fees, plus hundreds more in monthly membership dues. Also, many corporations no longer fund club memberships for mid-level management. Another factor is that competition continues to rise. Plus, members are demanding more and better services. Additionally, the exclusivity private clubs once stood for is no longer cool. And, when the recession in 2007 hit, dozens of clubs across the country went bankrupt or shut down. Also, baby boomer members are beginning to retire, but as far as gaining a new generation of members, the classic image of their parents' country club doesn't appeal to millennials or most of the young families of today. Another thing is that trends in dining have greatly changed from the traditional country club restaurant menu to healthier, more culturally diverse, and more casual offerings.

However, there are ways to turn all this around by embracing evolution. The industry is adapting by redefining and refining the organizations as communities rather than clubs...and communities that embrace and mirror the members of the local community in all their diversity. Also, by creating a more relaxed atmosphere, easing out-of-date rules, revamping the facilities, offering fitness and wellness centers, and more inclusive recreation, as well as embracing young families, including dedicating activities, events, and spaces for tweens and younger children, accommodating the millennials' attitudes and preferences, and increasing the club's appeal to women, who after all control most of the discretionary income in their households.

I have revitalized many clubs that I headed as COO and General Manager—rapidly taking them from red and black all the way to green. So, I wrote this book to share my hands-on know-how with you. Taking all the above and more into consideration, I wrote *12 Golden Keys to Hospitality Excellence* by drawing on my twenty-five-plus years of experience in the hospitality industry. I wanted to share my twenty-five years of dos and don'ts that make up these twelve winning business strategies, which can also be used in general and go far beyond the standard curriculum taught in hospitality or business schools. Each of these twelve keys is somewhat different than what most people would think about. Together, the twelve golden keys make a potent management formula. They are vital to successfully managing an operation, and applicable to any businesses, though in the book I emphasize the hospitality industry because it is my background. Still, as we all know, everything in business is about the people formula. At the end of the day, every business is in human resources—in the management of people and how to deal with them.

In business schools, they tell you the three important factors are people, process, and products. So, if you focus on people you develop process, then you begin working on products. But this book presents other perspectives. I think it will be an eye-opener for many business leaders, who by applying these twelve different business strategies can become winners in their field.

Now you are probably wanting to know a little about me. My life began in Casablanca, Morocco, where I was born the oldest of four children in a middle-class family—my father was an accountant and my mother was a housewife. I attended French schools and was a decent student. I was one of those kids who was not too concerned about his grades. Instead, as the class clown, I enjoyed saying and doing things that made everyone laugh. I remember when growing up, several of my teachers said in their reports that I was smart but too preoccupied with pleasing others and wanting to be noticed. My favorite subjects were mathematics, accounting (family legacy) and social studies. I grew up in an environment where most kids dreamed of becoming doctors, lawyers, engineers, and other white-collar professionals.

When I was fourteen years old, something interesting happened. My father wanted to purchase a business. He was an accountant by trade, but he wanted to be his own boss and become an entrepreneur. In a strange way, I still remember that scene when the whole family discussed possible business endeavors for my dad around the table.

Like many families, we came together at dinner each evening. The room filled with sounds of chatter and laughter as the spicy aromas of onions, garlic, parsley, cilantro, and saffron danced in the air. I sat at the kitchen table with my brothers, who were thirteen and four, and my nine-year-old sister, while my mom set a platter of succulent meat, a fresh, golden brown loaf of bread, and bowls full of bright colored vegetables on the table. Then she and my dad took their seats and each of us shared the day's events as we ate my mother's delicious, hot, homemade food. Dinnertime conversations were so fun, interesting, and happy, because our parents instilled the belief in all of us that everyone's opinion truly mattered, including the children's. On this evening, the whole family was engaged in a heavy discussion to determine the future of the head of our household. We were animated with ideas. Each of us laid our forks on our half-eaten plates of food or held them in the air midway to our mouths as we paused to brainstorm ideas of what types of businesses Dad would be best at and what would make him happy.

My mother attentively tilted her head forward and folded her arms on the edge of the table. And my father sat up straight in his chair with the keen alertness of an eagle, while his ears, eyes, and mind took in and digested every word we said. So, I felt like my thoughts and ideas...my words...had weight. It truly felt like the decision could be made as a family, as a team. It was, in fact, a great lesson that I frequently use in the boardroom these days. As leaders, we need to listen to everyone's ideas and then weigh and discuss them for the best outcome.

My father was looking at various existing businesses where he could use his skill sets, so while the family was discussing what kind of business he might launch, I asked, "Why don't you purchase a bakery?"

Everyone laughed. I wasn't taken seriously. Probably because they thought I wanted him to buy a bakery so there would be plenty of yummy crunchy almond cookies, sweet date truffles, and fluffy lemon cakes for us to eat. Another reason the idea of a bakery wasn't taken that seriously was that it lacked the panache of many other businesses. To him, it was an industry that required product knowledge and years of experience.

But what he didn't realize, and neither did I at the time, was that a bakery in a country like Morocco was a sure bet because everyone ate everything with bread. So, a bakery would almost never go out of business. It was a lesson I learned later in life.

When I came up with the idea of a bakery as a good business at fourteen, laughter ensued around the table because it didn't have the pizzazz of a big business, but what it did have was the assurance that if you put a little bit of money into it and you work hard at it, you will definitely make money and won't have any failures with it. After all, the purpose of any business is to make and keep customers, and to get those customers to bring in new customers and so on. The primary role of any CEO is to make sure the company doesn't go out of business. So, it's a huge stress reliever for any business owner or operator to have an enterprise with a product that is consistently in high demand because it's almost guaranteed to never fail. What my father didn't understand was that he'd be purchasing the existing staff and customers. He would have the opportunity to work on the team, streamline their processes and improve their products, but unfortunately, he didn't see it that way. He ended up purchasing an existing marble and granite company that made kitchen and bathroom countertops. He went out of business less than seven years later. Throughout my entire adult life, I questioned whether it was the operator, the operation, or even a combination of both.

So, I knew then, at fourteen, that I wanted to be an entrepreneur and work in an environment where I was always around people—having fun, seeing smiles on people's faces, and witnessing their family milestones like birthdays, anniversaries, bar/bat mitzvahs, and weddings. So, even then I knew I'd be involved in some type of industry that would allow me to be surrounded by people all the time. I'm not the kind of person who would enjoy being in the office for long hours. I want to walk around, meet people, shake their hands, and see how they're doing. So, I thought the hospitality industry would be a perfect fit for me, and I pursued that.

After high school, I decided to come to the US, where I attended a couple of colleges until I transferred my credits and earned my undergraduate degree at Adelphi University in Garden City, NY. Then, I decided to attain my graduate degree at Cornell University—an Ivy League institution, known as the best hospitably school in the world.

I felt a business degree from Cornell would open many doors for me in the hospitality field. That turned out to be an outstanding decision, because in 2017 Cornell merged the three schools, the Dyson School of Engineering, the hospitality school of Hotel Management and the Johnson School of Business, into one—the SC Johnson College of Business. So, if you have a degree from the SC Johnson College of Business, it ties you to the engineering school and the hospitality school. For me, it was an incredible opportunity to not only get a degree, but to get a degree from a school that is well-recognized in this industry.

I'm indebted to the caring, accomplished professors I've had over the years, who enriched my academic experience and provided me with a solid foundation for success. I'm also grateful to the dedicated staff, both employees and colleagues, throughout my career, who impressed and inspired me with their diligence and unrelenting effort as we worked side by side. I am thankful for the guidance and leadership of different bosses I've had. Every club president or owner I've worked for served as a mentor and role model, helping me grow into my full potential. Some of them are close friends and to this day we remain in touch and we continue to see each other a few times a year. We celebrate each other's milestones, meet for power breakfast or go out to dinner and even see each other during the holidays...like a true family. I never hesitate to call them for advice and I am truly grateful for their continued coaching, friendship and love.

And, for every job I have had, I felt I left it a little bit better than I found it. I aspired to always improve the situation, whether I stayed there for a few months or a few years. If, in my heart, I felt I was leaving the property in a little bit better shape than I found it, I was satisfied with the work.

My chief goals were to work towards the mission of the property, and each time to help at least one individual go back to college, get their degree, and better themselves. I'm proud to say that to date, I have influenced six individuals to go back and finish their degree. One of whom has already done so and is about to become a general manager as well. The other five are on their way, and God willing, they will be done soon.

I believe in hard work and perseverance. Most people, I can't say everybody, but most are given a fair chance and if they work hard and stick with it, ultimately, they'll reach their goals. What worked best for me to achieve a goal is to break it down into smaller ones. I never want to get discouraged from large, over-ambitious objectives. For example, when I decided to go back to school and get my graduate degree, it was scary to commit to another two years of school, because I was married with children at the time, and it was hard to go back. It's not easy to support your family with a full-time job, even one you love, while attending and studying for graduate school. It's a big load, but I kept my eye on the end game. The way I did it was to look at it as one class at a time and every other weekend. I had the support of my current employer at the time, and my wife and children, who gave me the confidence that the stars were aligned in attaining this goal. So, I did it. And, I felt good two years later, when I was able to say I held a graduate degree from an Ivy League institution. That was a major accomplishment for me.

So, with my goals in mind, along with hard work and perseverance, I continued throughout my career to become the chief operating officer of several prestigious country clubs in the metropolitan area, which is New York, Connecticut, and New Jersey. There I brought a record of success and expertise in strategic management and rapid turnarounds, building and optimizing highly effective business teams, developing cutting-edge campaigns that expanded the market share, and rapidly transforming struggling properties into market leaders.

The beginning (as a COO, obviously I had many other positions prior to that in other organizations while I was climbing the corporate ladder) was in Oceanside, NY, with the Middle Bay Country Club, set against the dreamy blue Middle Bay Harbor that shimmers when the sunlight shines from the clear, azure sky. I served as the Chief Operating Officer & General Manager of this 100-acre destination, featuring a 6,821-yard golf course of great greens and fairways, tennis courts, aquatic facilities, clubhouse dining as well as banquet operations, and a stunning 700-seat terrace with scenic water views. In all, I was responsible for an annual profit and loss statement of $5M, and a staff of seven who directly reported to me, in addition to my total staff of sixty permanent associates and forty seasonal ones.

There, I empowered membership development with an accelerated turnaround, improved financial controls, and implemented world-class standards—attaining seventy-three new members in year two, at an increase of 19 percent. Also, I dramatically boosted overall profits from a previous annual deficit of negative $500K to an impressive positive $800K. Additionally, membership development was transformed and accelerated with the tools and initiatives of the member-based marketing committee and the member recognition programs we established. Moreover, I spearheaded international recruiting and referral programs, as well as supported seasonal hiring through an H-2B staffing program (H-2B visa nonimmigrant program for temporary non-agricultural workers).

Following my tenure there, I advanced to the casually elegant Rockrimmon Country Club in Stamford, CT, featuring a spectacular eighteen-hole course designed by the famed, award-winning golf architect Robert Trent Jones, whose clients included Dwight Eisenhower, the Rockefeller family, and King Hassan II of Morocco. As COO, my team and I provided general management for the entire property, including a tennis complex, aquatics facilities, and a summer and youth camp program. Plus, we refined the food and beverage program for the three sleek and chic banquet and dining rooms. The Executive Chef and Food and Beverage Manager and I, across numerous member functions and social gatherings, escalated banquet sales by 10 percent in year one, and 9 percent in year two, with total food and beverage sales of $2.5M. Moreover, my team ensured the ongoing success of the organization by revitalizing this hidden gem as a top choice for golf events by orchestrating a range of high-profile affairs. We took the club from nearly zero bookings to hosting twenty major events and fundraisers, in addition to twelve golf outings. With the substantial boost in visibility and energy at the club, we brought in the new, millennial generation of members, and amplified bookings six-fold.

I managed the profit and loss statement with an operating and capital budget of $8.3M, and the strategic leadership of seven direct reports, ninety-five associates, and thirty seasonal personnel. I restructured departments and staff, created positions that focused on previously neglected opportunities, resolved chronic internal problems, and created new business opportunities.

Following those accomplishments, I moved forward to the Village Club of Sands Point in New York, one of the most vibrant clubs on Long Island. This former estate of the famed philanthropist, Isaac Guggenheim, faces Long Island Sound and is 210 acres of sprawling lush lawns, estate gardens, tall, leafy trees, and stunning waterfront views. The eighteen-hole course was designed by famed golf architect Tom Doak, whose courses rank among the best in the world. The one-of-a-kind Guggenheim Mansion offers formal dining and venue space for weddings and other special events. It also has two clubhouses, one of which, along with a new aquatic complex and tennis courts, were included in the range of construction projects and facility upgrades that I orchestrated.

Also, I, along with my entire team, fueled new member referrals by ensuring high-quality experiences and establishing a "Friends and Family" referral program. This work landed ninety new members, an increase of 12 percent. Moreover, I turned the EBITDA (an accounting measure of a company's earnings before interest, taxes, depreciation, and amortization) from negative $800K to a positive $200K. This streamlined inventory process decreased food cost from 54 percent to 38 percent and reduced beverage cost from 41 percent to 28 percent. Additionally, we partnered with the McMahon Group to develop a $26M strategic capital master plan. Before leaving, I initiated a $4M aquatic complex, $1M glass dome on the courtyard (reminiscent of Le Louvre pyramid) and $2M golf course renovation with seventy-three new Billy bunkers and a state-of-the-art irrigation system.

From there I moved into the Chief Operating Officer & General Manager position at the family-oriented and investor-owned Edgewood Country Club in River Vale, NJ, founded on a country manor estate, originally two historical Revolutionary War farmsteads. I was responsible for the outstanding social, recreational, and dining experiences the club offered to a growing dynamic, demographically diverse community of members. The panoramic fairways were presented in three distinct and gorgeous nine-hole courses—twenty-seven holes. I oversaw the full Edgewood Country Club operation, including the planning of the residential real estate component of 226 home sites. I mentored and motivated twelve department heads who directly reported to me, and a full team of 156 managers and staff. Additionally, I maintained financial responsibility for the club's $3M food and beverage program, along with overall revenue of $10M annually.

I am pleased and thrilled that this work did not go unnoticed. Throughout my rewarding career, I have always found it an honor to be recognized for my leadership and customer service skills, and for what I do every day. I've been distinguished with many prestigious awards and achievements including:

- I was awarded Visionary Leader in Club Management by Golf Kitchen in 2018

- I won First Prize at SC Johnson College of Business Shark Tank Competition at Cornell University in 2016
- I was recognized as Industry Professional of the Year by The Food and Beverage Association of America in 2014
- I was named Top Private Club President/Manager of the Year by BoardRoom Magazine in both 2010 and 2011
- I was honored as one of the 20 Most Admired Golf Operators in the World by Golf, Inc., in 2009
- I was recognized as one of the Top Guns in Club Management by Club Leaders Forum in 2008
- I attained the Rising Star Award for excellence in club management from the McMahon Group, Club & Resort Business magazine, and the National Club Association in 2006

I've also had the honor of serving on several esteemed boards and advisory appointments, including:

- The Dean Leadership Committee for SC Johnson College of Business at Cornell University
- Eric Caspers Food & Wine Scholarship, where I am the founding member
- The Metropolitan Club Managers Association, as a committee member

As you can probably tell, I really enjoy what I do—working as a COO in private clubs. I knew at fourteen years of age that a great business for me would be one that was there in good and bad times and would make others happy. Even though hospitality, in general, can be considered a luxury market, I look at it differently. During Hurricane Sandy in the New York area, when the clubs and hotels were destroyed, it was also a time when communities came together and came into the club.

Since the club had a generator, we were able to invite a

lot of people from the community to come in and take hot showers, recharge their phones, and eat hot meals—since the food we had in the refrigerators wasn't spoiled, due to the big generator we had at the time. So, we were able to offer shelter to a lot of people in the community. Those are the moments that are the highlights of hospitality businesses. We're not just talking about pleasing someone on a beautiful day. The best times are these extraordinary days.

For example, holding a golf outing to raise money for research for a cure for a killing disease, or raising money for the families who lost a loved one on September 11, or to raise funds for a family who just lost a child to suicide, so they can pay the funeral expenses. Those are the best times in the hospitality industry—when we can come together to help one another. I really enjoy doing what I do because of special days like that.

We don't get too many of those special moments in our lifetimes, but when we get them, we remember them forever. And, I'm in a field that gives me the opportunity to experience these moments more frequently than the average person.

In addition to serving as a COO of prestigious clubs, I now teach at Fairleigh Dickinson University as a professor in Contemporary Club Management. I like to give back and to teach others. I enjoy sponsoring kids to help them get to the next level.

I like promoting from within. Obviously, we try to give the opportunity to the best person who deserves it the most. But, giving the opportunity to someone from within your organization is a great way of showing appreciation to your current staff, and it also keeps everyone else motivated because it shows the rest of the team there is potential for growth.

More importantly, I love spending time with people and encouraging them to go back to college and finish their degree, because as far as I'm concerned, education is the most important differentiator that we can have. In a world where there is so much division and racism, education places everyone on the same level. It's not about the color of someone's skin or their origin, it's about how much they know, or how much they can bring to the table that levels everyone. I think that's significantly important.

My goal in everything I do is to leave it (the organization, the job, etc.) in better shape than I found it. If people read this book and say, "I feel I am a better operator, business leader, or hospitality leader," mission accomplished. If people feel they are in a better place than they were before they read *12 Golden Keys to Hospitality Excellence,* then I consider that a triumph.

Golden Key # 1:

You Can't Grow as a Leader if You Don't Develop Others

If your goal is to grow as a leader, stop worrying about your own development and focus on fostering leadership in others. The challenge of cultivating new leaders is a growth opportunity for you. Success is a spin-off of the leaders and mentors we follow, learn from, and confer with through our careers, as well as the people we groom and guide to leadership. One of the most important attributes of a winning leader is the commitment to helping others evolve and advance. It's a big responsibility, but very gratifying.

Developing Others

The best approach for advancing your career is helping others flourish in the workplace. As unreasonable as that may sound, you truly can't get ahead if the position or department you'd be leaving can't function without you. When you're helping others on your team build and shape their leadership skills, you're making it easier for the company to promote you. After all, if no one else can do your job, how can the company move you into another position? They'd be leaving an unfilled hole in that department. Also, if you're doing all the work and not delegating anything, you won't have time to develop yourself.

Train others to do your job, competently, so, you can move up in the organization. Higher management doesn't base your status and worth on your practical work, but on your expertise and the ability to build your team. While you're mastering new skills, delegate those new tasks with speed and efficiency in a way that positions you for long-term success. Effective leaders are aware of their staff's potential and they boost their team's growth and success. You will be rewarded for mentoring others by becoming a better leader and achieving a successful career.

Enabling

The key to a leader's success is their ability to enable their staff. Great leaders bring out the full potential in others. Every winning leader has a team of colleagues working together to take advantage of all opportunities and to solve all issues that come their way. Enabling is the opposite of controlling or dictating. It's only human to want to be captain of the ship or at least steer the ship where it's going. Everyone feels that way. That's why enabling works so well. It's a leadership behavior aligned with the way our brains function.

- However, enabling only works well when employees:
- Know what's expected of them
- Have the skills, know-how, and capability to fulfill those expectations
- Understand when it's necessary to ask the leader to remove roadblocks, provide resources and act as a liaison to other departments and members.

Here are some ways expectational leaders empower their colleagues to do their best:

1. They build from the employees' own strengths, leveraging their natural ability.
2. They develop their staff's ability to problem solve and make good decisions, both immediate ones and those for the long-term.
3. They help them increase their tolerance threshold

to handle more adversity, stress, and pressure. Also, they encourage them to take more risk and contribute more ideas. And, work with them on areas that need improvement, so they can rise to any occasion on their own.

4. They cultivate their staff's full potential by offering enough opportunities for them to gain the knowledge they need to succeed. And, they pair their colleagues with coworkers who are stronger, so they can learn from them and alongside them. By being surrounded by high-potential people, they will become top-notch performers.

Inspire

Successful leaders inspire commitment in their staff. Anyone with authority can use their power to command commitment. However, great leaders motivate their staff instead. Leaders can do this by mastering and implementing a few key leadership activities:

- Care. Colleagues who know they are appreciated show greater commitment to a leader's vision. However, when followers don't feel valued by their leader, they won't care much about their job. Demonstrate an unequivocal caring attitude to all your employees at every level. There must be no doubt that each one of your staff believes that you care about them. In turn, your team or staff will commit to ensuring that you don't fail.

- Create ownership. Ownership is closely connected to inspiring a shared vision. The level of commitment increases when people believe the leader's vision is also their own. Ensure that your employees can participate in discussions of how the work should be accomplished. Explain what each employee is contributing and the part they play in the task at hand. This enhances commitment and lets everyone know how important their individual role is to the completed project. When colleagues clearly appreciate their purpose in the endeavor, they will make a stronger commitment to the job.

- Ensure security. Employees are more likely to commit to a job and make more of an effort when they feel secure. For instance, if you encourage your staff to take calculated risks and make it clear to them that they won't be penalized in any way if they fail, they will give 100 percent of themselves to get the job done. However, if your organization doesn't tolerate failure, your team will hold back, reluctant to give their all. But, if your colleagues know you will stand up for them and defend them, they are more likely to share their knowledge and ideas and take risks that are essential for businesses to be successful. At Edgewood Country Club, I created a safe room, where anyone could say anything to a supervisor without fear of retribution. We celebrated mistakes and learned from them.

- Exercise accountability for everyone. Commitment and accountability are closely linked. When it's understood that everyone will be held to the same level of accountability, commitment is enhanced. A corporate culture of accountability supports collaboration, teamwork, and a willingness to have each other's back. When associates understand that everyone's contributions are essential to the success of the team, they're more confident, and will willingly share their knowledge, so everybody wins. If you enable your staff, your influence will reach far beyond your immediate department or team. Committed colleagues mirror their leader's vision because they are driven by the same goals. They act in their leader's best interests because they are committed to the same objectives.

Hospitality Leadership and Training Programs

A great way to develop others is to initiate a hospitality leadership training curriculum. It's crucial for general managers to develop their staff since country club professionals must possess a wide range of skills. In creating an effective hospitality leadership development program in a country club, we must consider the uniqueness of this segment of the hospitality industry. People join private clubs to get together for social and recreational activities with people who share similar interests, experiences, backgrounds, and professions. Typically, country clubs are owned by a sole proprietor or the members themselves. Therefore, their chief objective is to provide exceptional high-end service along with the finest properties, events, and amenities. In other words, private clubs are a people business, so clubs depend on their entire staff to have strong interpersonal and customer service skills. As a general manager you should take every opportunity available to help your staff strengthen their people and leadership skills.

With that in mind, one of the biggest challenges facing country clubs is high turnover. The loss of friendly, skillful, and talented workers can cause inefficiency, inferior service, complaints from members, lack of consistency, a reduction in sales, and the perception of ineffective leadership. To meet their major goal of consistently delivering world-class guest services, a country club needs to reduce employee turnover and encourage employee retention. Some benefits of leadership training and development programs are that they enhance recruitment, boost productivity, and foster employee self-esteem and job satisfaction, plus they cultivate a dedicated workforce, who stay with the organization much longer. When you involve your staff in the organization's culture and decision making, and further empower them by expanding their skills and knowledge, it boosts the overall success of the country club.

Management must embrace their leadership training programs. There is a direct link between a general manager's dedication to staff development and training and the effectiveness those programs have on the employees. A club's attitude toward training has a potent effect on the employees' motivation to step up and take full advantage of what's offered. There's no doubt, quality leadership is instrumental in staff development. Effective leaders help the staff attain their goals. Leadership development is a key element of a well-rounded hospitality education. Clearly, it's even as crucial, if not more so, than developing technical skills.

The way I see it, you only have two major tasks to accomplish:

1. Make sure that the business stays in business
2. Develop a succession plan for all positions

Golden Key # 2:

Over-Invest in People

"You don't build a business – you build people – and then people build the business." -- Zig Ziglar

Everyone needs somebody to believe in their potential and offer them a chance. After all, your business is shaped by the people you hire. They represent your club and are the key to your success. The best clubs consider their personnel an investment instead of an expense. Investing in your employees can cost a pretty penny, but it's more than worth it in the end. Your staff is your company's most precious asset. By investing in your workers, you're sure to reap an impressive yield. In other words, your employees are crucial to the success and viability of your club or company...and well worth the expense.

When your employees wake up each day eager to go to work, the excitement shows in their work performance, and your club will flourish. It boosts the momentum of the whole organization. When your club's culture nurtures your employees' development and success, empowering them with the freedom to be creative and focus on their most valued skills and capabilities, your club, in turn, becomes more successful.

Investing in your workers also enhances your rate of retention. When your staff loves their job and working with inspired colleagues, retention automatically follows. Additionally, you build loyalty in your workers when you acknowledge their value. It makes them feel supported, so they are more involved and dependable.

Company culture is regarded as the cement that holds a business together. By investing in your employees, you foster a culture that inspires honesty, reliability, drive, and collaboration.

Workers at companies who don't invest in them often feel unappreciated or overly criticized. And when employees are anxious and insecure, they get distracted.

We've all been at meetings in certain offices where the silence hangs so heavy you can't wait to get out of there, while at meetings in different offices, everybody's bustling with productivity. Management is responsible for tackling low morale and initiating an upbeat, thriving work culture, but it all starts with an investment in your employees. It's vital that you draw up a strategy to choose how you'll invest in your staff.

One element of that plan should be helping your employees with their personal brand. Workers' reputations distinguish them and promote a positive opinion of their attributes and skills. Effective personal brands empower your club's reputation as members of your staff represent it at events and conferences and by networking or participating in learning opportunities. When your employees are respected because they're active in the community or renowned for certain wisdom, talents, or skills, that positive perception extends to your club, advancing customer relations by bringing in new members and enhancing the loyalty of current members. Additionally, by bolstering your employees' online presence through social media profiles, blogs, and other content related to your clubs, it stretches your marketing reach.

Covering the cost of your employees' certifications should be part of your strategy. Having certified employees boosts your club's credibility and indicates how much you care about your members and that they can trust you to stay up-to-date with the latest standards and offer as much as, if not more than any other club. What's more, your certified employees can hold workshops for their team or the entire staff to share what they learned, which escalates the return on your investment in them. If it's a safety certification, you'll lower the cost of on-the-job injuries by preventing them. And, as many certification businesses will list your club in a searchable database along with all the companies they certify, your link with these credible organizations will enhance your club's reputation.

You'll also want to expand employee networks that rally talent and knowledge and boost exceptional performance throughout the organization or club. Create network infrastructures by assigning leaders to direct dialog and unite all ranks of employees in collaboration to share information and knowledge and to forge bonds, empowering management to align the vivacity of diverse employees to achieve company goals.

Your strategy should also include team-building activities to increase motivation, as well as:

- Reduce conflicts.
- Grasp the team culture
- Advance efficiency and output
- Strengthen social and communication skills

In addition, offering other perks and benefits shows how invested you are in your employees. A rock-solid benefits package differentiates your club from the competition, and both attracts and helps you retain top talent. WellCare benefits help your organization lower its health care costs and reduce the expense of absenteeism. Plus, healthy employees are at their best each day.

Your plan should also involve developing your staff's leadership skills. The most productive and prosperous businesses produce their own leaders with leadership development. Also, most employees are loyal to and stay long-term with companies that provide that career path.

Another element of your strategy should be to provide your workers with the latest in technology. You will draw in new employees and retain current ones if you give them modern technology that helps them excel. Attending to the technological needs of your staff shows you're committed to their comfort and success. State-of-the-art technology can propel your club forward and help you attain your goals.

If you're looking for high-quality, key ways to invest in your employees, here are some major ones:

- Hire the Best
- Always Train
- Overpay to Avoid Sabotage

Hire the Best

Invest in hiring the best person for your club. You must put in time and money, but your club will save funds they would have lost in turnover, lost sales, lost members, and employee theft if you'd hired the wrong people. Hiring is about acquiring employees who are the best fit for the job. To do that, your hiring practices and day-to-day operations need to be directly aligned with the club's values. Also, you must be able to describe the duties and control points of the position that you're interviewing for. So, design jobs based on what your club needs and target the right candidate. Usually, the best applicants come from referrals.

Once the position is defined and you know the type of candidate you want, here are four major qualities to look for:

- Competence – Center on what the candidate

accomplished at the previous club they worked in regarding improving operations, impacting the services provided to the members, or how many people they mentored. Most likely they'll repeat their work performance in the past in their new job at your club.

- Attitude – Anyone can learn skills, but warmth, honesty, courtesy, enthusiasm, and friendliness, which employees of a private club critically need to deal with members and co-workers in the best way possible, aren't easy to teach.
- Integrity – Look for displays of ethical behavior in their previous jobs as well as honesty. Interview any senior level candidate at least three times and ask the same questions, including those regarding important values, to see if the answers are consistent. Typically, when honest applicants are asked the same questions several times, they'll basically answer them the same way.
- Compatibility - The candidate's management style should be compatible with your club's culture. Some key points to observe in the interview are how well they articulate their thoughts, their body language, including eye contact, and the types of questions they ask.

Always Train

Limited growth and promotional opportunities are key reasons why numerous employees leave their country club positions. Creating a culture that supports training and development provides a monumental payoff in the end because it's a lot less expensive and more efficient than replacing them.

When a club upgrades their workforce's skill set through company training, it heightens the staff's productivity and motivation because they know management appreciates them. Since you care about your employees' growth and advancement, they care about their coworkers and the growth of the club, and in turn, they work even harder.

Training provides your entire staff with the skills and tools to succeed, thereby increasing club productivity and profitability. Also, training encourages your staff to spread their knowledge. When employees are taught new skills or better ways of doing their job, they want to share what they learned with the team. It also motivates them to imagine ways to improve procedures. The advantage of acquiring new skills is also an effective reason for seasonal workers to return.

Cross-training ensures employees are flexible, efficient, and capable in more than one aspect of the club. It's also beneficial when it comes to scheduling and filling in for absences, plus it cultivates team spirit since employees understand the challenges their co-workers face, especially in seasonal operations as most clubs are.

Training and instructive programs challenge employees and keep them engaged. By giving your staff greater responsibilities, exciting projects, and the opportunity to advance, they'll work at a higher level.

Through ongoing training, your employees will advance their technical aptitude and skills and keep up with hospitality trends and innovations. Enabling your employees' development ensures you're creating future leaders for your club who are adept at inspiring growth, change, and innovation.

Training is also a recruiting tool. Potential employees will grasp that you want to help them grow with the club. This will impress job applicants as well as members. Remember, club members prefer to join a club that invests in their employees over one that doesn't.

Additionally, promoting from within your club to executive positions is smarter than hiring externally. Internally promoted employees usually perform at a level that far surpasses those who were hired externally. Also, external hires are usually up to 20 percent more likely to resign. When you have a good training program, it's much easier to promote from within the company.

Moreover, employee development programs make it easier to determine the strengths and weaknesses of your employees, so you can assess which ones are management material. After all, a management position should be filled by an employee who has been with the club for a while, is well acquainted with the business of running a country club and has attained continuous training and advancement there.

For the simple cost of a training program, you get a capable and industrious staff to amplify and accelerate your club's success—now that's a bargain.

Here are some ways to start your training program:

- Your training program must meet the needs of the employees, department, organization, and club members. Feedback from a country club's employees and members is crucial in creating a winning training program that is practical and easy to apply to day-to-day tasks and situations. A good training program will boost the club's bottom line and fix any gaps in the team.
- Get management involved. Come up with classes or lunch meeting lectures taught by leaders in the club. Also, encourage your leaders to take classes so they can then share what they learn with their team. Choose a warm, hospitable space that expresses your business culture to use as your training room.
- Establish training goals and add a segment to your regular employee review forms for notes about

discussions and advice regarding learning.

• Also, club leaders should write training manuals for their staff where you continue to share the club's mission and vision, to help them carry the torch.

Overpay to Avoid Sabotage

Numerous clubs spend 55 percent or more of their revenues on payroll because they know that hiring a remarkable staff will pay off by creating an outstanding experience for their members. Employees shouldn't be thought of as a cost but as an asset. The club's high expectations and service ideal, as well as the value you place on employees, must be mirrored in the wages you pay. To recruit the best of the best you must pay employees the highest income reflected in the market. Approximate the top salary each worker could make in a similar position at other companies and pay the maximum.

The only advantage to frugally compensating your personnel is cheap labor costs, but the benefits of paying your employees well are boundless.

Here are six reasons to overpay your employees:

1. You can entice and retain remarkable employees by offering equally remarkable compensation.
2. You'll be compensated with devotion, high morale, and engagement if you show your employees that you prize them more than revenue.
3. Employees who are paid well are productive, but an employee who is unhappy with their wages and is looking for a better job isn't productive at all.
4. Members prefer to join clubs that are good to their employees. Also, if an employee feels underpaid and unappreciated, they won't care about their job and might be rude, snappy, or curt to the members. So, paying low wages will lower your club's

reputation and credibility.

5. When you pay liberal salaries, you can raise your expectations and hold your employees to a higher standard. And, they raise the bar for themselves to excel in the position.

6. To stop your competition from poaching your best workers one by one, giving them a tremendous advantage over your club, only because you chose to pay low wages. If you don't pay your employees what they're worth, another club or organization will.

Use Emotional Currency

Nowadays, it takes more than just money to inspire workers to give their all at work. In addition to better salaries and perks, modern workers want to grow and develop their roles. Country club employees spend long hours at work, so their job is more to them than a place to go to make money. They look at their company, the club, as their community. It's a significant source of social support to them. Also, when your staff feels secure, respected, and valued, and find meaning in their work, they're more likely to create and contribute fresh, innovative ideas and take risks.

What your employees want even more than they want a raise or promotion is:

- Pride in what they do.
- A life apart from work, some time to spend with friends and family.
- Fairness. Nobody wants a job where the bosses' favorites are rewarded and recognized over those who work harder and achieve more.
- Coaching and help when needed without any micromanaging.
- To be heard, for their contributions to have value, to have some say or influence in the club.

- Less stress. They want to work for a club that plans, predicts potential problems, and sets realistic goals, so they don't stress out their employees.
- Some job security. Though they don't expect lifetime employment, they don't want to feel that at any moment they may be let go or the company may close.
- To be on the winning team. Employees want to help their company beat the competition.
- A boss they can respect—a leader worthy of their loyalty.
- Challenges. They want to contribute to projects beyond the normal scope of their duties, to avoid tedium and help the club succeed.

So, you can see that when you invest in your employees, they will drive your company to success. It's an investment your club is guaranteed to reap rewards from.

Golden Key # 3:

Celebrate Diversity

The world has shrunk due to globalization, and as the people move across countries, cultural differences like belief systems and values become an everyday factor in business. Cultural diversity is fundamental to the hospitality industry, which is filled with people of different ages, races, and cultures. However, there's still room for improvement. It's important in the hospitality industry to empathize with people of diverse ethnicity and cultures. Many hotel chains transfer managers overseas to destinations with cultures profoundly different than their own. But even if your hospitality employees only work in the US, the American consumer base and its workforce are more diverse than ever before. Hospitality businesses must effectively acclimate to the diversity of both their markets and employees. Monoculture companies, on the other hand, are disadvantaged by their limited perspective.

Let's look at the primary and secondary differences that make up diversity.

Primary variances are age, race, gender and so on. Secondary differences are less obvious and include a person's values, religious and political beliefs, level of education, sexual orientation, marital status and their experiences. These less visible traits also affect our perspective. Both the primary and secondary features of each individual employee have some impact on your business. Additionally, cultural diversity can be linked to multiculturalism—in communities with multiple cultures, no one culture predominates. Interculturalism is when two cultures interact. But, in multiculturalism, several cultures engage. I strongly feel that the hospitality industry makes it easier for different ethnic groups to work together and remain focused on the tasks at hand. The best example that comes to mind is the Disney philosophy where everyone plays a character regardless of their origin or background. Everyone contributes equally to the success of the operation from the CEO to the janitor. I regret not having worked for Disney, as I truly love what the company stands for.

Diversity is good business and good for employees. A variety of skills, experiences, and cultural understanding in your organization gives you a competitive edge in the hospitality business in many ways:

- Diversity increases retention and reduces absenteeism by boosting employee loyalty
- When your staff learns to appreciate others' views, it increases their interpersonal skills and boosts their abilities as team players.
- The company gains from a wealth of different experiences and viewpoints.
- It provides a multidimensional approach to innovation
- You'll form a superior workforce by attracting the widest selection of candidates
- Diversity boosts a company's profitability and value in the global hospitality market
- In companies that embrace diversity, more employees feel empowered to attain their full potential, fueling motivation and performance
- Supporting diversity cultivates an adaptable, receptive corporate culture
- A diverse staff's capacity to communicate across cultures is an asset in anticipating and satisfying customer expectations
- Successful diversity management enhances your

team's creativity, choices, and results
- Diverse staffs can be highly effective at complex tasks because they provide information, skills, critical analysis and different perspectives
- Diversity reinforces continuous improvement, which enhances profitability, productivity and returns on investments
- By hiring employees who are fluent in other languages and cultures, you remove barriers with your clientele and attract more international guests
- Diversity can help your customers feel more comfortable by giving them more opportunities to deal with employees who are more like them
- Diversity creates more effective teams. Studies conclude teams with diverse cultures, abilities, and knowledge excel over teams where members have the same skill sets
- A multicultural workforce provides a variety of viewpoints, which enhances a company's decision-making process

Everyone in the workplace should feel welcome and empowered to express themselves so they can contribute at their highest level.

Diversity Training

Sometimes workers feel puzzled or confused when facing diversity, and that can interfere with the smooth running of your company or even the level of service your customers receive. It's vital to instill an awareness of cultural diversity among hospitality employees. Diversity training is the answer, and it has been proven to increase performance. Successful diversity instruction also results in creating your own in-house experts. Many US hotels and restaurants are employing diversity education at all levels of their businesses, so their staff will accept coworkers and customers who are from different backgrounds.

Having diversity leaders and the support of upper management make it easier for workers to welcome diversity training. Train your personnel to skillfully interact, collaborate, and work with people who have different cultures, beliefs, and abilities. Diversity training will also ensure that employees understand culture at individual, national, and organizational levels.

There are three major aspects of diversity training:

1. Looking at things afresh
2. Contemplation
3. Insight

There isn't one class that can teach employees how to properly engage with people from different cultures. Provide all your employees with a complete training program on diversity when they first join your company and follow up with refresher courses. This empowers your workers to accept others and to work with and help them in a respectful and courteous manner. It also inspires your staff to encourage employees to speak up for each other, which cuts down on intolerance. Also, consider having a cultural diversity expert empower your employees with a presentation or lecture. Additionally, language and cross-culture-gap training is essential in the hospitality industry. Language and cultural barriers are a strain on communication between employees, and moreover, they can create misunderstandings, affect teamwork, and reduce morale. But employees can expand their knowledge and skills in dealing with people from different cultures with language and cross-culture-gap education. Consider holding quarterly cultural training sessions to assist your staff in initiating better ways for teams to manage workplace diversity. You might want to provide implicit bias training, which makes it easier for people to realize and admit they're making choices swayed by cultural inclinations, and sometimes unconscious leanings. Also, establish incentives among teams to spur employees to solve issues and develop projects together, as well as initiatives like celebrating global traditions. You can also merge diversity training with your already-established training program.

Also, diversity training should be implemented in all levels in the hospitality industry. Along with interactive cultural and diversity training, establish additional courses for management on topics like how to build an inclusive team or resolving diversity conflicts. Also, cross-cultural training for managers helps them handle cultural diversity issues better, and it diminishes the potential of expensive mix-ups or misunderstandings caused by cultural differences.

Use diversity trainers who are accommodating and accomplished in managing conflict and group dynamics. Take the various methods of teaching into consideration, including videos, quizzes, workbooks, role play, small group work, or creating and participating in class skits to determine which ones might work best in your staff's training. It's essential that trainers gauge results and are accountable for them. Assessments can induce employees to focus on the topic that leads to results.

However, diversity training isn't enough. There needs to be a strategic plan on how to implement diversity in each department and function in the company.

Diversity Management

Hiring a multicultural staff and honoring their differences is just a start. You need to embrace diversity management as part of your business vision, illuminate its value, and inspire inclusion and different opinions. Managers and executive teams should commit themselves and lead by example, and the company needs to provide the resources to make it work.

All hospitality businesses need a complete, collaborative, and reasonable diversity plan that is measurable, so it can be tweaked as needed. Then, management needs to create an effective timeframe for executing the plan.

Diversity management demands a deliberate effort to foster a pleasant, inclusive work environment. Managers need to create an environment of honesty, openness, and equality, so employees are comfortable expressing their ideas and opinions. Therefore, it's vital that companies employ managers from both marginal and mainstream sectors who back diversity strategies and are determined to lead their multicultural workforce to success.

Successful management takes diversity from a legal necessity to an asset for their company, employees, and customers.

For customer satisfaction and loyalty, managers need to adapt their services and amenities to the varied preferences of multicultural guests.

As far as your employees go, modify your policies to ensure cultural inclusion and an accepting environment for your staff. Meet with each employee at least once to get to know them individually, which will also prevent stereotyping their staff, plus it makes employees feel valued. Also, managers need to be aware of the perceptions and differences in the various subgroups in their workforce. They can then take that knowledge and integrate all that along with their employees' needs and values into their diversity plan with programs like teaching certain languages, or involving families in some company activities, which all adds to an inclusive atmosphere.

Managers need to make sure their employees use respect

as a guiding principle in all interactions with coworkers. And, that they're aware of differences in age, race, beliefs, physical traits, sexual orientation, and that such things don't diminish anyone's contributions to the workforce. Additionally, managers should coach veteran employees to mentor new hires.

Managerial skills, practices, and styles need to be upgraded to provide better leadership to a spectrum of employees with different abilities and perspectives. Diverse workforces benefit from different styles of management. Some workers prefer a more hands-on style, while others do better with basic direction and working independently. But, it's important to get feedback from employees so you can make sure they have everything they need to do their job and that they're treated fairly.

Also, part of diversity management is initiating a strategy for your business' future regarding spotting and cultivating a diverse pool of potential leaders. In addition, the recruitment process and human resource management plays a chief role in diversity leadership. The Human Resources Department's equal opportunity policy should reward an employee based on their contributions to the workforce, and not take their age, race, gender, culture, religion, or any other characteristics into consideration. HR management should ensure that all managers and executives integrate diversity policies into all sectors and occupations in the company. Their fundamental task is to create a culture that fulfills the business' cultural diversity plan.

It's imperative to put an open-door policy in place to encourage reporting. If employees experience an inappropriate or illegal situation, they should tell their supervisor, someone else in management, or human resources. Company policies should ensure employees won't be retaliated against for reporting serious concerns in good faith. If such behavior is reported to a company, they need to document and investigate the allegation. If it is found that an employee did violate the policy, or any laws, disciplinary measures should be taken, depending on the circumstance: a refresher on the code of conduct, a verbal warning, a written warning, suspension, or termination. Businesses can consult with employment attorneys to make sure they're in full legal compliance before taking adverse action against an employee.

Keep in mind, diversity management entails promotions, leadership, and employee incentives.

Challenges

It is challenging to manage a workforce with different traditions, values, holidays, and manners. Many companies face challenges in managing diversity and find it difficult to overcome them.

Some of the challenges and even barriers to diversity in a company are:

- Racism, sexism, ageism, and homophobia are challenging factors that can prevent a business from reaching its goals.
- Majority and minority cultures don't always have similar experiences.
- There are always employees who will reject cultural diversity and its changing patterns.
- Cultural diversity also complicates decision-making because of all the different viewpoints.
- Changes in values affect people's thoughts and actions, which often result in conflict.
- Some employees don't adapt well to change
- People who do not share cultural values have greater difficulties in understanding each other.
- Employee differences enhance the potential for

conflicts and misunderstandings.

- When most employees oppose a change, the effective change will not be accomplished.
- Cross-cultural challenges arise from cultural gaps.
- Communication is a huge challenge for culturally diverse organizations due to perceptual, cultural, and language barriers.
- Some people purposely use language to exclude people from certain groups.
- Employees feel loyalty to their original cultural background groups rather than to the whole organization, which affects commitment and loyalty to the company.
- The principles of ethical decision-making certainly differ for the employees of the organization with different values, beliefs, and rituals.
- Here are some proven ways to overcome diversity challenges:
- Expose unconscious biases. Humans naturally associate with people who are like them. But by standardizing practices we can eradicate predispositions from the hiring process and company policies.
- Use a buddy system for coworkers who have noteworthy differences (an experienced worker with a newbie or a local employee with one who moved here from a distant state or country), so they'll get to know each other. Switch up the pairs on a regular basis so all the employees get a chance to work closely with each other.
- If you have many employees who speak English as a second language, encourage all your employees who are native English speakers to learn key phrases in their coworkers' primary languages. Consider using a translator service to transcribe the company handbooks into other languages.

- Overcome stereotypes that certain types of people are good or not good at certain things, such as the idea that Asian men are good at science and math and women are not, or older people aren't good at computers and younger people aren't reliable.
- Practice inclusion to bring employees who isolate themselves or are isolated by others into the mainstream, highlighting their skills and achievements so other employees can appreciate their work.
- Many new hires won't automatically adapt to your workplace culture, so you need to mentor your employees in welcoming diversity.
- Employ sensitivity training so your staff will learn that all human beings share basic desires, like taking pride in their work and being valued and needed.

A good way to discover the challenges you are up against, as well as any improvements made, is through assessments and evaluations. They are a vital means for management to measure what's going on in their workplace. They'll show you the current progress of your diversity plan. Also, they can help companies decide what inclusions to add. They can be based on workforce statistics, customer service surveys, or even complaints. Gathering information from managers about the cultural diversity goals and challenges they deal with is another type of strategic assessment. You can also use focus groups made up of managers, supervisors, and employees to assess the barriers and issues associated with diversity in the company. All these methods help identify challenges and offer guidance regarding diversity in the hospitality industry.

Reassessments are important to long-term evaluations and advancements. Initial assessments can act as benchmarks for later ones. For example, a business can execute an employee survey on diversity for a reassessment to attain information from the whole workforce. To get the most out of reassessments, you should look at both the process and the results. Comparative analyses of other organizations are also great assessment tools.

It's more important than ever to meet the needs of diverse coworkers and guests and avoid any friction and frustration as much as possible. However, companies do need to regulate the numerous challenges regarding diversity.

In conclusion, the many similarities between people from different cultures and backgrounds will help them get along and work well together.

Celebrate your employees' differences. Encourage them to share their unique characteristics and viewpoints. Help develop a workplace that promotes fairness and inclusion. The H2B program brought us students from several countries, so we decided to hold a talent show and an international dining event where buffet tables were set up around the periphery of the room and the students represented their countries with their national dishes. It was a huge success and it definitely created a sense of camaraderie and fraternity.

Golden Key # 4:

Embrace Change

Change is constant in the hospitality industry and it impacts customers, members, managers, and employees. You'll notice a variety of changes in rates, staff, menus, events, brands, analytics, management, guest/member expectations, job responsibilities, revenue strategy, distribution, technology, and industry mergers. Businesses need to engage in active transition and restructure their company around new processes.

Here are some examples of just some of the changes in the industry:

- Networks like Expedia, Travelocity, and Kayak have pretty much supplanted conventional travel agencies
- Airbnb, Homeaway, Flipkey, and Vbro are innovative and popular options to traditional lodgings.
- Even well-known classic brands have undergone mergers and acquisitions
- Millennials have driven the development of fresh hospitality brands with novel ideas
- Private clubs aren't relying on golf as the chief draw for everyone, they're adding other amenities like fitness centers, yoga classes, biking groups, marathons, teen game rooms, climbing walls, and so on.

Change is a gift—it grants new chances for companies to benefit from shifting demographics, innovative tech, or the latest markets. However, challenges also arise from changes like more competition, workforce shortages, and defining moments.

To embrace change, take a fresh look at the full scope of it as well as the current climate. You'll be able to identify coming changes if you take a creative approach by initiating new ways of doing things and innovative ideas.

These tips will help you succeed and take advantage of the opportunities change offers:

- Appreciate that not only is failure essential to learning but that along with risk-taking, it is the key to success.
- People are inspired by their colleagues' ideas and accomplishments, so foster a collaborative environment—which is also known for raising a team's group IQ.
- Positive thinking encourages your employees' creativity and boosts success.
- Humor goes hand-in-hand with productivity and innovation. It's conducive to unique ideas and lessens stress. Teams that laugh and have fun together are more creative and prolific than more serious, quiet ones.
- Brainstorming generates numerous ideas, motivates the team, and encourages a non-judgmental environment.

Paradigms

A paradigm is a typical example, model, or pattern. Paradigms like division of roles and responsibilities bolster positive service performance, which ensures memorable guest experiences and generates profitability for owners and investors. But when a paradigm changes, it basically erases the old rules and boundaries and we must adapt to new ones. We must look at things differently. Depending on our background, perceptions, or beliefs (cultural and otherwise), we can be intimidated or frustrated by shifts in paradigms. After all, we had a set of rules, a pattern, that we followed for years and suddenly someone or something completely changes it. It's human nature that when our regular way of doing things changes, we're fearful and resistant to that change. These paradigm shifts are the reason for most of the issues and chaos that come with change.

These paradigm shifts of disruptive innovations, shifting global economies, climate change, employee and societal demands, and changing consumer preferences can radically shake up regimented business structures. But changes can be advantageous. As Albert Einstein said, "In the middle of difficulty lies opportunity." This is particularly important to me as I mentioned earlier with Hurricane Sandy and what we did for the community.

People who are optimistic about new ways of doing things are prone to benefit from the opportunities they offer. Typically, those who accept change and moreover are enthused by it are successful in business. I remember how the industry resisted wearing denim in the dining rooms. Members used to say that is was not clubby enough, it was too casual. However, as soon as they adopted it, dining reservations went through the roof and overall, member satisfaction was at an all-time high.

In the hospitality industry, changes can sneak up on you, so keep that in mind when it happens. You have a choice of anticipation or alarm. Though no one can foresee the future, those who prepare for changes are more likely to look forward to them.

Here are some shifts that are revamping the relationship between hospitality employees and their customers:

- The Internet—Interaction with the Internet has accelerated to the point that the average American spends twenty-four hours a week online. So, it's vital that your business is up-to-date on online trends in your target market to improve communications and build visibility, which will increase occupancy, customer loyalty, and operating performance. Your social media presence is crucial to your continued success.

- Mobility—Hospitality businesses should employ mobile devices for interaction and to individualize the customer experience. Eighty-four percent of people access the Internet from mobile devices. Also, use mobile access to connect with, engage, and motivate your workforce.

- Expectations—Each year customers' expectations increase, and these new demands propel the hospitality industry.

- Generation Gap—Many private clubs have relaxed their dress codes because younger members found them too restrictive. Also, they have waved rules on tweeting and texting on the golf course, for example, which turned off younger members. So, by relaxing the dress code (members don't have to tuck their shirts in and some even play music in golf carts), and allowing cell phones on the fairway, younger people are joining. At the same time, the older members, who prefer the more traditional ways of doing things, can still abide by them, but by personal choice rather than rules.

Though paradigms are essential and beneficial, they can negatively impact business by obstructing novel ideas or solutions. Hospitality companies that are willingly open to new perspectives and opportunities, and immediately respond to paradigm shifts, tend to thrive.

Overcoming Opposition to Change:

The resistance to change that companies encounter can be categorized as:

- Organizational—Threats from unknown or unwanted organizational form and process change and intimidation prompted by the internal or external business environment.
- Group—Threats to team cohesiveness and social standards that will spark resistance to change if they aren't correctly handled.
- Individual—Personality factors that level various emotional responses to change.

It is essential that management resolves to lead the change. Employees are a company's most valuable resource. Managers need to consider them and involve them in the process, as well as resolve to lead the change. But, spurring on your hospitality workforce is not a simple mission, as every employee has a unique personality and outlook. Managers need to voice their new vision clearly and positively. Throughout the change, they must make sure that information is shared through all communication channels and understood and adapted by the entire staff.

Employees need to be kept up to speed on all future changes since they're the ones who'll be incorporating them. They're your front line, the ones your customers will be looking at and talking to when they ask about the change.

Managers also need to ask their staff for feedback regarding the change. It's crucial that managers utilize their active listening skills before, during, and after the change is implemented. They need to hear their staff's opinions and understand their views and appreciate their perspectives on the changes.

When workers don't cooperate with their superiors or collaborate with coworkers, the level of service provided to the customers goes downhill. Additionally, when employees resist change, conflicts can happen with managers and colleagues.

Employees might not put forth their best work, which can harm the company's reputation. And, some employees might even quit. To prevent all that, management must realize that they need their workers to be onboard with the change and ready to employ it. In turn, management needs to actively show they back the change and they support their staff.

Continuous change in the hospitality industry is necessary for survival. Hotels, clubs, restaurants, and other businesses that stay stagnant and don't improve will have a hard time keeping up with competitors. A cheery workplace is vital to change. Happy, motivated employees have a friendly rapport with coworkers, which lifts morale and improves performance, and that raises customer satisfaction, which keeps the company profitable.

Employees often benefit from one-on-one coaching, with their manager or supervisor talking to them about the hurdles that are hindering successful change. When a worker opposes change, their direct superior is best able to zero in on which part of the change they don't like and help them deal with it.

When managers and employees share the attitude that there's always room for improvement, it's easier to effect change, which keeps the hospitality industry moving forward into the future.

Technological changes

Embracing innovation, rather than resisting it, impels businesses to grow. The hospitality industry has come a long way from the days of a cash box instead of a cash register. Plus, we now have mobile payments and much more. Private clubs and other hospitality organizations need to utilize new technologies to make it easier to meet the distinctive expectations of their members. For businesses in this technology-centric industry to succeed, they must embrace change.

When you begin to utilize the latest technology, you need to help your hospitality staff adjust to the changes. It's vital to develop your strategies and plans before the change. Create a smooth transition by initiating the changes without impeding your employees' regular tasks.

Naturally, change comes with uneasiness and doubts, but once your staff understands what it entails, plus the benefits, it will be easier to enhance your business with innovative technology.

Here are some of the latest technological changes or ones to be prepared for:

- Bots—Chatbots can be programmed for any language and they reply to more customers at once, multiplying the number of leads and the volume of business over what you'd get without them. Some prominent hotel brands utilize robots as a virtual concierge or at the front desk for answering questions, telling customers about local tours and recommending various eateries, activities, and sites to see near the hotel, and to handle basic room requests via the logistics system. Private clubs can use them in the same way to provide information on activities, schedules, and upcoming events, and to respond to any questions. Chatbots improve efficiency and reduce costs by handling these basic tasks and quickly answering guest or member questions, plus they operate 24 x 7. Of course, for those members who want to talk directly to a person, staff is always on hand. But for most members when it comes to general information they prefer the speed and convenience bots offer.

They also provide a way for companies to easily evaluate interactions with customers to understand members' or guests' preferences, which helps the staff provide more personalized services.

- Tech-Enabled Meeting Spaces—Modern meetings run on technology. Business people need to make multimedia presentations and video conference remote attendees—sometimes both simultaneously. And for marathon meetings, they want access to services like catering with minimal interruptions. Most of all, clubs and hotels know they need these spaces to be as user-friendly as possible. The A/V rooms of the past that required dedicated engineers are no longer an option. If you think these kinds of business needs are limited to boardroom-style conference spaces, you're missing an important part of the picture—business customers are increasingly asking for advanced technology enablement in ballrooms and event halls as well.

- Mobile phones—Hotel keys are expected to become data in guests' cell phones either through NFC technology or by scanning a barcode. Private clubs are using cell phones and other mobile devices to take food and drink orders and handle point-of-sale transactions, which is more efficient and therefore frees up some of the staff's time, so they can provide more individual, personalized attention to the members.

- Voice Platforms—Siri, Bixby, Google Home, and Alexa, are all commonplace now, and they're getting smarter all the time through machine learning. People use them daily to set alarms, play music, regulate household devices and more. They're also useful in the hospitality industry. In hotel rooms, guests can use them to control the lights, drapes, television, do not disturb notices, and the thermostat. Voice technology is also often used in clubs and hotels for booking, taking simple food orders, and performing other mundane tasks so the staff can devote their time to more meaningful interactions with the members or guests. Housekeeping staff can use them to confirm which rooms or areas have been cleaned or need to be cleaned. Voice-activated platforms are easy to use and can be customized to a company's needs and preferences. Going forward, companies in the hospitality industry are sure to change many current procedures by incorporating this technology in new ways.

- Blockchain—Booking systems and review websites, for example, can be greatly enhanced with this technology. Blockchain could connect customers to hotels without requiring large commission fees. Also utilizing blockchain means that clubs, hotels, and other hospitality businesses have an option of taking cryptocurrency payments, which don't require transaction fees. It's also anticipated that in the future disputes can be automatically solved by using smart contracts.

- SIP-DECT—is popular in the hospitality industry in Europe, as a mobility-enabling alternative to wireless broadband networks and radio-based networks for managers and staff no matter where they are on the property. Even if they are in areas where cell coverage may not be good, like the golf course, they can be contacted. It can also be used in hotels to reach the valet, concierge, and more. It's economically reasonable, especially compared to the alternatives, easy to use, and offers a predictable voice quality.

- Data Explosion—Vast data is gathered through

mobile bookings, guest reviews, Internet search engines, and other means. When it's analyzed, it helps hotels, clubs, and other companies drive buying behavior, stay ahead of trends, as well as develop target pricing and customer loyalty programs. The data lets businesses know which programs, promotions, and discounts specific customers will like the best. For example, it can be utilized to pinpoint which item on the menu card will sell best in specific holiday seasons, customize email updates, target coupons specifically to guests' preferences, based on their past purchases.

- Self-help—With wireless self-service kiosks, club members can order their meals right from the golf course. When they finish their round of golf, their dinner will be ready to eat. Also, remote check-in and check-out options are becoming popular, and in some hotels, guests use apps on their cell phones for room service. In private clubs a spectrum of services can be automated, which frees the staff up for activities that better enhance the member experience. And the trend is only going to accelerate.

- Apps—Guest apps fuse everything from announcing specials to features to loyalty programs. Private club members can use a virtual concierge app to book tee times, restaurant reservations, or to learn about upcoming events. If a customer uses the group rate for a conference, a hotel can use the app to message them information on the event with a map of meeting rooms where sessions will be.

- Digital Signage—With WLAN, clubs and other hospitality businesses can post menus, schedules, promotions, announcements, club news, tournament scoreboards, and so on, anywhere on the property.

- Virtual Reality—VR changes the way hotels, clubs, and other hospitality businesses are marketed— going beyond images, text, and audio-visual ads. Customers can view golf courses, swimming pools, spa and fitness facilities, conference rooms, restaurant dining areas, and even nearby tourist attractions almost as if they were there. Customers can use virtual reality to see what their stay would be like or what being a member of the club would be like. Virtual reality can be utilized to tell a compelling story and give customers an experience they'll enjoy while promoting a company. I see this as a major tool for membership recruitment.
- Augmented Reality—With new advancements in augmented reality, the hospitality industry will be using it more in the future. There are AR apps that guests can use to virtually redecorate their hotel room. AR games allow guests to make their location an important part of an established AR game. AR can be used with interactive elements in a hotel room like AR wall maps. Customers can make their own apps, which can make exploring the hotel or locale more enjoyable.
- Tech Lounges—are stylish spaces that offer wi-fi and a place to check in, access local info guides, relax, or get work done in a spot other than their room, and they are great for private clubs as well.
- Biometric Authentication—This technology will allow members to leave the club restaurant after they eat, knowing their bill is automatically paid though there's no wait staff or pay terminal interaction. The smooth processes of getting purchases verified immediately, in the golf shop or hallway house (Food & Beverage Service Area at the Turn) for example, without using money or even

using a phone or wallet, digital or otherwise, is convenient for members. It can be used the same way at hotels. However, this is one of those changes that some consumers will probably resist due to privacy and security concerns.

- Radio Frequency Identification—If members have RFID tags on their cars, the staff will know the moment they arrive at the club, which will improve the level of service. Also, they can be used for security purposes and to track golf carts, golf bags, and other belongings and property.

- Location Based Services—Members of a club or guests of a hotel can get service no matter where they are on the property. The staff can locate members any time and any place in the club or hotel to deliver services to them. It also works the same way when you need to locate employees, so it increases the efficiency of hospitality businesses.

- Unplugged—Another big change is some hospitality companies are embracing detoxing or unplugging from tech. The idea is that if members or guests aren't online, texting or scrolling through social media, they'll use more amenities and have a more peaceful and relaxing time.

Technology like AI, AR, and biometrics raises us to new heights of serving customers. We live in an era of never-ending change. Employees who are flexible and can easily adapt, and managers who are skilled in leadership, will pave the way to new innovations in the hospitality industry. One of my favorite examples is when I introduced the usage of electronic on-the-spot mini surveys in the restaurants. As you can imagine, in the country club industry, everyone is an expert on food and every member wishes to design the menu the way they'd like it. It was very powerful for me to have live data where I could have a conversation with a member the next day who would say, "I hated my steak and I can bet you that everyone felt the same." I had the data to know that it was not the steak because 98.6 percent of the members and guests who had the same item the night before clicked that they were very satisfied with it. As we are trained to make the customer happy, I would always find a clever way of making her happy without blaming the steak.

Golden Key # 5:

The Power of Social Media

Like many other industries, the use of social media in hospitality has become vital. Nowadays, it is almost impossible to get the word out without a well-structured and well-thought-out campaign through several platforms. It's no wonder social media marketing is a topic that has gone viral. After all, 4.02 billion consumers are online. The average person spends two hours a day sharing their opinions and reading those of other people on Facebook, Twitter, Instagram, and other social networks.

But those aren't the only sites they use. Yelp, Urbanspoon, and TripAdvisor are also popular for connecting with others who share like-minded interests and values. Furthermore, collaboration-hospitality has evolved because consumers want new and unique experiences. They no longer base decisions on brand loyalty. Popular people-serving options such as Airbnb are transforming the hospitality industry.

Reviews at these various spots allow consumers to learn about experiences others have had. People trust social media reviews by friends, family, and associates and even total strangers more than they do those from news stations or ad agencies.

Once consumers see online reviews and ratings that are like their own experiences, they begin to rely on the opinions on these sites as if they were posted by a trusted friend or family member. They make choices on dining, travel, entertainment, and leisure activities based on that feedback.

The power of social media lies in actively participating on social networks and encouraging customers to share their opinions, since they are more believable to other consumers than advertisements and their reviews can reach further.

Many hotels and airlines have launched their own online communities to replace their previous rewards programs. Since monetary value is a key element in drawing new customers, many of these online travel communities provide discounts or coupons to encourage nonmembers to participate. Businesses who have a lot of active members on these sites are often successful in building long-term relationships with their customers. These sites usually offer specific benefits such as providing travel information, booking reservations, setting up tours, listing feedback on the level of customer service they provide or the ambiance of hotels or restaurants, and allowing members to share their own experiences with others in the community.

There are many strategies you can use that are targeted at specific online communities:

- Post daily.
- Display your social media links on your website.
- Also, advertise them in emails, blog posts and at your business where your customers will be sure to see them.
- Take the time to write trendy, beneficial, and exciting content to receive a high number of impressions from the social media channels' algorithm-based newsfeed.
- Also, follow your customers and members on social media and encourage them to follow your Instagram, Facebook, and Twitter accounts.
- Track the number of discussions or comments about any new service or benefit you're offering or

that anyone in your industry is.

- Reply right away to reviews, comments, and feedback, and resolve customer issues quickly.
- Make the most of the real-time info on market trends and consumer needs that social media platforms offer to revise your advertising or plan new services, amenities, or events based on that info.
- Pay attention to your customers' comments and feedback to see if your offerings fit what they want and discover what features you offer that they like the most.

Twitter

The 284 million on-the-go users on Twitter come there for whatever's fresh, thought-provoking, and timely. The 6,000 tweets keyed per second come to about 500-million daily. Also, you'll find five times more new videos there than any other platform.

For Twitter, you want to keep your page updated frequently. Also, carefully craft your bio to instill your brand's persona so tweeters feel like they know your company and like it. In addition, your bio has the dual purpose of getting followers, so you can build customer relationships with them and get them to do something, so you want to include a call of action. Also, try to fit in two hashtags. Put the best photo possible with your hospitality business bio. In addition, it's vital to include your location. Consumers enter the location they need in their tweet searches and if yours isn't listed, your hotel won't pop up in the results. Fitting all this in when you're allotted a maximum of 160 characters is hard to do, so be creative.

As for tweeting, be sure to mention that guests who book directly will get the best deal and tweet any promotions you're running. Also, create private lists in Twitter so you can target your marketing to a selective group of users.

In 2017, Twitter expanded its character limit to 280 for tweets. But it's still a short space, so you want to make the most of it. Include a link to your website in your tweets. It's easy to shorten your link for that at *tinyurl.com*. Links are great for tweets because 92 percent of all Twitter users click on them. Adding a link is the simplest way to get more views and shares.

Hashtags

At Twitter, hashtags rule—they stretch your tweet's reach, and steer potential customers your way while building brand awareness, customer engagement, and loyalty.

Here are some tips on how to use hashtags:

- If your business is a hotel, you can generate leads by using the hashtag for specific events, concerts or festivals coming to your area in a search along with the word—hotel. Most likely tweets from people searching for lodgings will pop up.
- To foster brand awareness, use any trending hashtags suitable to your business, especially those for local landmarks, tourist attractions or hotspots near your hotel.
- You can also connect with and support local companies by following them and tweeting about their services to your followers. They will repay the favor.

Using the right hospitality hashtags is the key to stretch your reach and increase engagement. The obvious one is #hospitality, but here are other popular hashtags below if your business is a hotel:

#pool

#hotel(s)

#resort

#5starhotel

#hoteldeals

#besthotel(s)

#luxuryhotel

#bedandbreakfast

#boutiquehotel

#luxurytraveller

#skiresort

#vacationhome

These are just some samples of hashtags you can use. Good hashtags will result in new followers and more engagement. You also might try these examples of travel hashtags:

#trip

#travel(s)

#holiday

#tourist

#beach

#seashore

#mountains

Along with the travel hashtags, use your location such as:

#NYC

#London

#LA

#Hollywood

#washingtondc

Here are more popular hospitality hashtags:

#countryclub

#golf

#privatecountryclub

#golfcourse

#restaurant

#tenniscourt

#athleticfacilities

This gives you an idea of the kind of hashtags to use. Feel free to play with the Twitter search bar and try different words with a hashtag in front to find the best ones for your business. Again, you should use location hashtags with them and your brand hashtag. If you don't have a hashtag specifically for your business, create one and encourage members or customers to use your brand hashtag. Ensure that it fits your club and isn't already used.

Try using a mix of general and niche-specific or brand-specific hashtags. But keep in mind that the hashtag is minor compared to your content, it's the quality of your tweet that's crucial in making an impact. Also, when it comes to social media, don't overlook Facebook.

Facebook

After the Cambridge Analytical scandal, Facebook made several adjustments to boost privacy and transparency. Beginning in January 2018, Mark Zuckerberg revamped newsfeeds to greatly reduce organic brand content and support more friends and family posts. Also, they began phasing out third-party data used for target marketing. And they've made a lot of updates, not just the ones that let users modify privacy settings and delete their data, but other ones as well like Facebook's new augmented reality ads, which will help them hold onto their competitive edge. However, it's notable that a study released in September of 2018 shows that 44 percent of users in the eighteen to twenty-nine age group deleted the Facebook app from their phones in 2018. Compared to the sixty-five-and-older users who deleted their Facebook app, the ratio for the younger users leaving is four times more.

Moving forward on Facebook, you should develop a unique marketing plan that connects your business objectives to the consumers' wants and needs. You can use Facebook stories, live, images, videos, and Facebook ads. Post gorgeous, high-quality photos because images drive 2.3 times more interaction. Also, Canva and Picmonkey let you easily enhance your pictures by adding text or graphics. Videos also catch consumers' attention, if they have captions, are accessible, easy to understand, and the gist of it is useful or valuable. Add links to share company news and your blog articles. It's advantageous to use Facebook's live content because it triples engagement. Consider using Facebook stories, they're trendy and are placed in top position on the newsfeed.

For Facebook ads, consider applicability and cost-effectiveness. Assess what works best to foster awareness. Make certain the ad conveys your brand message and showcases your facilities, logo, and business colors. Let the viewers know what you can offer them that other companies can't. Ensure it upholds the tone of your Facebook page. And, include a specific yet easy call to action.

Facebook groups are great places to mingle and share videos, photos, and comments with others who are customers of your business or have similar interests. Members can also upload photos to the group album, ask "Friends" to group events, and message others in the group regardless of "Friend" status.

Secret groups are great for promoting club activities and functions to members. Administrators should encourage interaction by promptly liking posts and responding to them. The group administrators are the ones who choose who can join the group. There are three types of groups:

Open—Anyone viewing the group can see the members' posts. They can also see them in newsfeeds or searches when they join or receive an invitation to join.

Closed—The posts can only be seen by members. But the group name and its members' names are visible to anyone on Facebook.

Secret— The name of the group doesn't show in Facebook timelines or searches. Nonmembers can't see the group name, member list, or anything about the group.

Secret groups are great for promoting club activities and functions to members. Clubs can also create sub-groups like mini-clubs for engagement on specific topics or special events.

Besides setting up your own Facebook group, another way is to search groups for those relevant to your hospitality customer base, such as those for travelers, golfers, tennis players, and so on. Join these groups, and be sure to follow any rules against promotion, then use them to discover the latest content related to the industry and to share content with your prospective customer base.

Since Facebook ad content is highly visible, people see it frequently, so update and revamp it every week or two.

Make a spreadsheet to record your core metrics so you'll be aware of what you want to accomplish with the ad. Look at your click-through rate to determine where you can improve.

Here are tips on the best times to post on Facebook:

- The best day is Thursday
- Highest engagement —12 pm to 2 pm on Wednesdays, and from 1 to 2 pm on Thursday.
- Other good days and times to post—between 10 am to 3 pm.
- Saturday has the least engagement

And as far as times—early mornings and late nights have the least engagement.

Interaction is the key to success on social media, and it's easy to get your staff involved by creating an employee advocacy program. Provide your staff with shareable content that shows everyone you're not just another hotel or club. Your reach will spread much further with content shared through your employees' feeds. Posting videos is an easy way to get people engaged with the hotel, club, restaurant, or other hospitality businesses. Post any events or celebrations you hold on the property or nearby. Personalize your company by posting pictures or videos of the Christmas tree or your staff in Halloween costumes. Speaking of pictures, consider including Instagram in your social media strategy.

Instagram

Instagram is the leading photo sharing portal, boasting 200 million active users. It's an essential platform if you're reaching out to millennials, as 90 percent of Instagram users are under age thirty-five. It's also perfect for hospitality businesses to engage with users.

Check out the images and hashtags your competitors are

using there, so you can see what does or doesn't work. Consistent, enticing images attract customers, and with the variety of filters and layouts they offer, you can vividly showcase your property's top attractions. Use hashtags including those for locations. Also, routinely enter searches for photos guests have posted of your hospitality business. And don't forget what a great addition blogging is to any social media strategy.

Blogging

Blogs offer a lot more space than social media sites to share anecdotes that build interest in your club, restaurant, facilities, accommodations, or nearby tourist attractions. Furthermore, well-written, catchy, compelling posts draw potential guest to your website. For branding, include your logo and company colors on your blog. Share your blog posts across other social media platforms.

Regularly update the content so readers will come back often, which will boost your online visibility. Since Google indexes everything online, your blog is another way to bolster your cyber presence. Websites with a blog receive about 434 percent more indexed pages. Also, all hospitality businesses should keep TripAdvisor in mind for social media marketing.

TripAdvisor

TripAdvisor is a chief source of ratings and reviews for hotels and all types of hospitality businesses. Your media team should stay on the lookout for any reviews, particularly less favorable ones, and reply within one hour. Offer your guests review cards featuring TripAdvisor, Yelp, or other platforms to encourage them to share their experiences. Also, don't forget what an important part videos play in your social media strategy.

YouTube

With 1.8 billion YouTube users logged-in each month, your social media strategy should embrace videos. Over half of YouTube views come from mobile devices, reaching people everywhere. And, 67 percent of viewers are likely to make a reservation after watching a virtual tour of the hotel or club. Be sure to use popular keywords in your title. Create a catchy and detailed description and include your property's website link and phone number. Also, another great social media network you want to consider is LinkedIn.

LinkedIn

The biggest professional network connects over 500 million people worldwide. Through several hospitality groups on LinkedIn, you can easily network and exchange ideas and strategies for building your social media presence.

Also, LinkedIn videos for sponsored content help you build brand awareness and drive traffic to your website or use videos on your business page to spotlight your news and events. LinkedIn is another place where you want to use hashtags in your posts. And don't overlook Pinterest as a major social media platform.

Pinterest

Pinterest is a perfect fit for the hospitality industry because it has 70 million global users and is a favorite of foodies and travelers. Many major hotels and clubs, value it as part of their social media plan. When creating your page, focus on your profile picture and the details: company bio, website link, and the boards at the top, because they're the sections that capture most people's attention.

The idea behind Pinterest remains simple yet ingenious.

It's like the old-fashioned cork bulletin boards we used to pin things on. The general rule of thumb is a minimum of ten and a maximum of fifty boards. Make them as general or as specific as you want. Pick a topic for each board and a category. People with similar boards are likely to re-pin your pictures. Choose catchy but clear board names and appealing board covers. Pin photos of your hotel, club or hospitality business, along with images of local landmarks, plus vacation or leisure-time activities that are popular in your area. Post a brief SEO enriched description and a link to your website with each picture.

Tips for Clubs

Social media is a great marketing tool for private clubs. First, by engaging on the various social media networks in the same ways we've gone over. Secondly, consider running sweepstakes or contests to get people excited and involved. Some great prize ideas are a free thirty-minute tennis lesson, a round of golf or a dinner for two at your restaurant. Contests also enable your business to gather leads and referrals, plus they cultivate brand loyalty.

Another idea is to point out a picture-perfect spot for a selfie (maybe on the golf course) to share on social media. Also, consider displaying scrolling feed in your clubhouse so everybody can see the posts about your club on social media.

Social Media Teams

If you remain proactive, responsive, and keep customers updated, they'll use your business again. So, it's essential that you form a friendly, dedicated social media team that responds immediately to all feedback and prompts positive reviews. On Twitter, for instance, 78 percent of consumers expect companies to respond to their complaints within an hour. Take every review and comment seriously. If you don't respond to complaints or unfair criticism, it can diminish the positive feedback you get.

Also, most customers post questions they have for a company on its social media page. If you assist them as promptly as you would if they were standing at the front desk, your brand will build the trust of consumers and you'll soon have a base of loyal customers.

It's clear that all hospitality establishments such as hotels, restaurants, apartments, private clubs, hostels, and all others can build their business and increase profits through the power of social media marketing.

Golden Key # 6:

Be A Student of the Obvious

"They were simply horse-sense analysis of situations, and then more horse sense in the working out of a plan."—Robert Rawls Updegraff

When it comes to marketing you can't be too obvious. After all, the definition of obvious is—easy to understand, evident, and standing out. Those words alone tell you why an obvious strategy is so powerful... and why it works so well.

The best book ever written on using an obvious marketing strategy and on marketing in general is *Obvious Adams - The Story Of A Successful Businessman,* by Robert Rawls Updegraff. Though published in 1916, over a hundred years ago, it's still 100 percent relevant today. First published as a column in *The Saturday Evening Post*, it featured a character Updegraff created named Obvious Adams, a copywriter in advertising. Adams was authentic and down-to-earth yet got amazing results from ad campaigns by going with the obvious rather than what was clever or brilliant. He tackled a different advertising challenge in each installment of the column and always managed to hit on the obvious answer, which had everyone shaking their heads and saying, "Why didn't I see that?" His gift for coming up with perfect yet obvious solutions every time earned him the name Obvious Adams.

The column was all the rage with its frank and simple business advice that marketers could apply right away to ads or issues they were working on.

In pursuit of answers and tactics, we're liable to dismiss

what is right under our noses – the obvious. The advantage of an obvious approach is it's simple and easy to explain and work out, but those are the same reasons it doesn't appeal to many clubs or other hospitality businesses. A lot of clubs want a brilliant, not-so-obvious wow factor in their advertisements. Many marketing, clubs and other companies often look for the creative, instead of the obvious, with advertising designed to entertain rather than to sell. They seem to go for getting laughs or generating shock value. To these clubs and marketing agencies, it's about theatre more than it's about marketing. It's about the gimmick more than it's about selling.

However, when it comes to communicating a message to your members, imaginative and brilliant can come across as vague, dreamy, or distant, as well as confusing, which makes for an inefficient and unsuccessful marketing campaign. So, don't look for complex solutions. Look for simple solutions to complicated issues. Think innovation rather than creativity.

Think of it this way: logical points are forceful, convincing, persuasive, believable and clear. Doesn't that sound like points you'd like to have to support what you're selling? Those seem like points you can use to overcome most objections to close a sale, don't they? Yet, how many logical points or arguments have you found in contemporary marketing? I bet it's hardly any. A shortage of logic is at the core of why many campaigns fail. Yet, countless advertising professionals abhor the idea of a marketing strategy that isn't based chiefly on creativity. So, in turn, they don't like obvious ideas. Still, the most effective ideas show members a clear reason to join your club or consumers a concrete reason to buy your products. Now, that doesn't mean an obvious advertisement has to be bland, you can also be obvious in a dramatic or innovative way. But, keep the reason to buy your products or join your club utterly logical and obvious.

If you didn't know already, I'm sure you're getting the idea now that seeing the obvious is a specific marketing strategy. To come up with the obvious approach, Adams-like, we or anyone must employ several common-sense methods that pay off. To become a student of the obvious that Adams was, we and the staff at your club also need to be:

A Hard Worker: Adams worked hard. He committed 100 percent of himself to everything he did. He was thinking and revising, night and day. As Robert Rawls Updegraff wrote, "Thinking is the hardest work many people have to do, and they don't like to do any more of it than they can help. They don't gather all the facts and then analyze them before deciding what really is the obvious thing and thereby they overlook the first and most obvious of all business principles."

For example, in the story, as Adams is alone at a table in a restaurant eating dinner, two men enter, sit at another table to eat, and begin talking about Adams. The following passage is from the book:

"Ordinary-looking man, isn't he?"

"Yes, to look at him you would never think he was the famous Obvious Adams of the biggest advertising agency in New York. And to tell the truth, I can't see why he is such a little tin god in the business world."

"I've heard him speak two or three times at the Adleague meetings, but he never said anything that we didn't know already. He seems to have a lot of people buffaloed, though. I confess he was a disappointment to me."

But the whole time they're talking about Adams, he was

making business history. He had turned the menu card face down and was drawing lines and making notes on the back. To anyone looking over his shoulder the result of his work would have been meaningless, but it seemed to please Adams, for he nodded his head earnestly to himself and put the menu into his pocket as the obsequious waiter came to help him into his overcoat.

Observant: To be a student of the obvious, you must pay attention. Robert Rawls Updegraff's character, Adams, is keenly observant—far more so than the other copywriters. I don't think any of them even bothered tasting the cake for the cake campaign.

Here is an excerpt on that from Obvious Adams:

Before any orders came through to the copy department some of the copy men got wind of it, and Adams heard them talking about it. That day he spent his noon hour looking up a grocery that sold the cake. He bought one of the cakes and ate a liberal portion of it as his lunch. It was good.

That night when he went home, he sat down and worked on the cake problem. Far into the night the gas burned up in the little third-floor-rear room. Adams had made up his mind that if he had a chance at any of the cake copy, he was going to make good on it.

The next morning the cake business came through to the copy-room. To Adams's great disappointment it was given to one of the older men.

He thought the matter over all morning, and by noon he had decided that he was a chump forever thinking that they would trust such copy to a kid like himself. But he decided to keep working on that cake account during his spare time just as though it were his account.

Three weeks later the campaign opened up. When

Adams saw the proofs of the first cake copy his heart sank. What copy! It fairly made one's mouth water! Preston was famous for food-product copy, but he had outdone himself on this cake. Adams felt completely discouraged. Never would he be able to write such copy, not in a million years! Why that copy was literature. It took mere cake at fifteen cents the loaf and made it fit food for angels. The campaign was mapped out for six months, and Adams carefully watched each advertisement, mentally resolving that he was going to school to that man Preston in the matter of copy.

Four months later, in spite of the wonderful copy running in the newspapers, both city and suburban, there were mutterings of dissatisfaction coming from the Golden-Brown Cake Company. They liked the advertising; they agreed that it was the best cake advertising that had ever been done; it was increasing the business somewhat, but sales were not picking up as they had anticipated. At the end of another month they were more disappointed than ever, and finally, at the expiration of the six months, they announced that they would discontinue advertising; it was not so profitable as they had hoped.

Adams felt as keenly disappointed as though he had been Mr. Oswald himself. He had become very much interested in that cake business. On the night he heard of the decision of the Golden-Brown Cake Company to stop advertising he went home downcast.

That evening he sat in his room thinking about Golden Brown Cake. After a while, he went to a drawer and took out a big envelope containing the ads he had written for the cake months before. He read them over; they sounded very homely after reading Preston's copy. Then he looked over some street-car cards he had laid out for his imaginary cake campaign. After that he *assembled a new carton he had drawn out and colored with water-colors.*

He sat and looked at these things and thought and thought and thought. Then he fell to work revising his work of months before, polishing it up and making little changes here and there. As he worked his ideas began to develop. It was nearly three o'clock when he finally turned out his light and went to bed.

The next morning, he went to the office with his mind firmly made up as to what he should do. At ten o'clock he telephoned the front office and asked if he might come down and see Mr. Oswald. He was told to come ahead.

Updegraff goes on tell us that Adams got that campaign and he shows us why with the following passage:

They all agreed with him in his contention that people ought to taste the cake, and that to supply grocers with sample slices wrapped in oiled paper fresh every day for three weeks to give to their customers, was a good idea; that his idea of showing the cake in natural colors in the street-car cards where it would, as he expressed it, "make people's mouths water," was a good move; that giving up their old green package in favor of a tempting cake-brown carton with rich dark-brown lettering would make for better display and appeal to the eye and the appetite.

Analytical: In *Obvious Adams*, the owner of the ad agency says of Adams, "He doesn't get carried away from the facts; he just looks them squarely in the face and then proceeds to analyze, and that is half of the battle. "

Adams would observe the product and circumstances, compile the facts, study them, and from all of that he concluded what the obvious choice was. For instance, in the book, a company with two hat stores in a large city had success with one but not the other and they couldn't figure out why. Whenever they ran an ad campaign, the thriving store prospered but the other store's sales never improved at all. So, Adams studied the store to find out why it had low sales.

Here is an excerpt from the book:

Adams was surprised, when he found the store, to discover that he had passed it three times while he was looking for it! He stood on the opposite corner and looked at the store. It had only a very narrow front on Market Street, but a very large display window on the intersecting-street side. He stood thinking. It struck him that that store was too hard to find. What if they did do heavy advertising — he knew of the Monarch campaign in that city—the other store would reap the benefit because it was so prominently located, even though not right on Market Street. Yes, he felt sure this was the unprofitable store.

As he stood watching the store, he began to notice that more people went up on that side of the street, which meant that as they approached the store their eyes were focused ahead, watching for the crossing policeman's signal to cross, and as they did cross the intersecting street their backs were turned to the big side window. And even those who came down on that side of the street did not get a good view of the window because they were on the outside of the sidewalk, with a stream of people between them and the store. He counted the people for periods of five minutes and found that nearly fifty percent, more were going up on that side than were going down. Then he counted the passers on the other side and found that nearly fifty percent, more were going down on that side. Clearly, that store was paying almost twice as much rent for that side display window as it should, and Market Street rent must be enormous.

People didn't see the store; people couldn't find the store easily.

That night he thought, figured, and drew diagrams in his hotel room. His theory seemed to hold water; he felt sure that he was right. The next night, after having studied the situation another day and obtained some rent and sale figures from the store manager, he took a sleeper back to New York.

A few months later, as soon as the lease expired, that store moved.

A person who knew what they wanted and acted: Be frank and straightforward about what you want. Ask for what you want. For example, in the story, Adams goes to the agency and requests an interview with the owner of the company himself. When the secretary says Mr. Oswald is too busy to see him, Adams doesn't say, "I'll try another day," or ask for an appointment, he says, "I can wait for an hour and ten minutes." He is then told that Mr. Oswald will see him in twenty minutes. The president of the agency meets with him and is not impressed and sends Adams packing. Before leaving, Adams tells the president, "Well, Mr. Oswald, I have decided that I want to get into the advertising business and that I want to work for you, and I thought the obvious thing to do was to come and tell you so. You don't seem to think I could make good and so I will have to set out to find some way to prove it to you. I don't know just how I can do it, but I'll call on you again when I have found out. Thank you for your time. Good-bye."

Oswald is suitably impressed by this attitude and he offers Adams a position at his firm. Twenty years later, Adams advanced to vice president and acting leader of the Oswald Advertising Agency. After you ask for what you want, follow that up with action toward that end goal. Don't let opportunities pass you by because of a preconception or because you were too timid to go directly to the source. Don't sit around doubting your ability. Instead, set goals and plans of action to prove your ability. Decide what you want, and what you need to do to get it.

Persistent: Never give up. Don't let anybody or anything keep you from the path you know is meant for you. If you really want a task that has not been assigned to you, don't wait to be given the project, work on it on your own like Adams did when the company got a new brief from a peach canning company. Here is an excerpt on that from the book.

He thought, studied, dreamed, and ate peaches, fresh, canned, and pickled. He sent for government bulletins. He spent his evenings studying canning. One day he sat at his little desk in the checking department putting the finishing touches on an advertisement he had written and laid out. The copy chief came in to ask him for the back number of a certain paper that was in the files. Adams went to get it, leaving the advertisement on top of his desk. The copy chief's eye fell on it as he stood waiting.

"Six Minutes From Orchard to Can" was the heading. Then there were layouts for pictures illustrating the six operations necessary in canning the peaches, each with a little heading and a brief description of the process:

California Sun-Ripened Peaches

Picked ripe from the trees.

Sorted by girls in clean white uniforms.

Peeled and packed into the cans by sanitary machines.

Cooked by clean live steam.

Sealed air-tight.

Sent to your grocer for you — at 80 cents the can.

The copy chief read the ad through and then he read it through again. When Adams got back to his desk the copy chief—Rowland by name—was gone. So was the advertisement. In the front office, Rowland was talking with the president, and they were both looking at an ad layout on the president's desk. "I tell you, Mr. Oswald, I believe that lad has the making of a copy man. He's not clever—and goodness knows we have too many clever men in the shop already—but he seems to see the essential points and he puts them down clearly. To tell the truth, he has said something that we up-stairs have been trying to say for a week, and it has taken us three half-page ads to say it. I wish you'd apprentice that boy to me for a while. I'd like to see what's in him."

"By George! I'll do it," agreed Mr. Oswald.

Aware of his Audience: You are advertising to your members and potential members, not your competitors. Focus your message to your audience, your present and future members. You need to make it obvious to your members why they should join your club. Show them that your club has everything they've been looking for and need, even if there are other clubs with the very same amenities or features that also fulfill their needs and desires. You aren't marketing for other clubs, you are marketing your club to prospective members.

For example, when Adams was drawing up a campaign for a bond paper company, he researched the way they made paper for two days, then presented tentative ads to the president of the paper company based on his study. Here is a passage from the book on that:

"Every good bond paper is made of carefully selected rags "—quoting from the advertisement in his hand; "every good bond paper is made with pure filtered

water; every good bond paper is loft-dried; all good papers are hand inspected."

This is an excerpt from Obvious Adams of what happened regarding that bond paper campaign:

"Mr. Merritt, we aren't any of us paper-makers, and no one has ever told us these things. I know there is nothing clever about these advertisements. They are just simple statements of fact. But I honestly believe that the telling of them in a simple, straightforward way as qualities of your paper, month after month, would in a comparatively short time make people begin to think of yours as something above the ordinary among papers. You would be two or three years at least ahead of your competitors, and by the time they got around to advertising, your paper would already be entrenched in the public mind. It would be almost a synonym for the best in bond paper."

Mr. Merritt was evidently impressed by the logic of Adams's argument, yet he hesitated.

"But we should be the laughing-stock of all the paper-makers in the country if they saw us come out and talk that way about our paper when all of the good ones make their paper that way."

Adams bent forward and looked Mr. Merritt squarely in the eyes. "Mr. Merritt, to whom are you advertising— paper-makers or paper-users?"

After the column came out, Robert Rawls Updegraff published Obvious Adams as a small book—short story size. That book is now in the public domain, which means it is no longer copyrighted in the US, so it can legally be shared in full or in part as I have done here, and easily read for free. Here is a link where you can access it along with some of Robert Rawls Updegraff's other books. http://onlinebooks.library.upenn.edu/

You are probably wondering why I chose this key. I sincerely believe that most answers are usually right in front of us. I think that every leader should see, taste and feel what their customers experience. I strongly believe that it is important for the staff to use the club, hotel or resort (when appropriate) to truly see it from the members' or customers' point of view. It is imperative to allow staff to play on the golf course as well as use the fitness center and dine in the restaurants. Some might see it differently, but I respectfully disagree. After all, how are you supposed to improve something without first-hand experience using it? The idea, as mentioned earlier, is not to abuse it and to only utilize the facilities when it's appropriate.

Golden Key # 7:

Member Satisfaction in A Club Environment

The crucial task, from the general manager down to the hourly staff of every country club, is to keep the members happy and satisfied. As a member-driven service organization, it's vital that clubs focus on customer service and satisfaction. Even more so now, since across the country, clubs are facing declines in membership and fewer potential members wanting to join. General managers and CEOs are challenged to increase member loyalty and retention rates. The industry expanded globally in the latter part of the 20th century, and numerous new clubs and golf courses were constructed. Soon there was too much of a good thing, too many country clubs, because it intensified the competition between clubs, adversely affecting operations and driving many to decrease dues and initiation fees.

This motivated some clubs to switch their focus from recruiting new members to retaining loyal ones. Also, retaining current members is easier and less expensive than acquiring new ones. It costs five times more to bring in new members than it does to keep current ones. It's also easier to satisfy the wants and needs of current members because the general manager and the staff are familiar with their preferences and behavior, but it takes time to learn what new members like or don't like. Additionally, new members sometimes must be lured away from other country clubs with incentives, which are an added expense.

Another benefit of retention is that members spend more

at the club the longer they've been there, and they refer others who become members. Also, happy, devoted members are more willing to pay higher fees.

Satisfaction occurs when members' expectations are met or surpassed. In fact, to foster member loyalty, you should constantly try to exceed your members' expectations. Research has found that longtime, loyal customers are those who are delighted with the quality of service and the facilities. Also, your efforts to satisfy your members and in turn cultivate their loyalty should start from day one with a commitment to provide superior personal service. The staff should learn the members' names, favorite dishes, activities, likes and dislikes, so they can deliver individualized service and make them feel special. Personalization is vital to cultivating happy and loyal members. Their satisfaction is essential since your club's success and reputation rests in their hands.

Satisfaction occurs from either the club meeting the members' needs and desires or from an appraisal system based on their experiences as active members of the club. Crucial factors that influence a member's decision to renew or not to renew are:

- How active they are in the club
- The quality of service, and
- The value they do or don't feel the club offers them.

Value

Perceived value is also an indicator of whether a member will be satisfied with a club. Additionally, it's a chief reason why potential members do or don't join a country club. General managers need to deliver great value to draw in and hang on to members. For example, since many golfers join and use a country club, the club's worth is strongly related to three qualities:

1. The viability of the course's design
2. The quality of its upkeep and maintenance
3. The quality of the experience of golfing on it

Also, in general, offering a variety of activities and amenities can increase your members' and potential members' perception of the value of your club. After all, to satisfy their members, clubs must meet their needs and wants. Beyond golf, a club can enhance its value to members by extra amenities the competition doesn't have.

Many clubs add value to their club with a world-class spa and fitness center, offering everything from massages to tailor-made exercise programs with personal trainers. Offering health and fitness classes for children and teens, like hip-hop dancing or yoga, provides more value to those with family memberships. So, the quality of the spa and fitness center is a value that can be utilized to attract new members and hold on to current ones. Additionally, when it comes to dining at the club, members value acceptable prices as well as high-quality food and service, and when these are provided, they're another reason people join or renew their membership.

Also, to be of value to members, club managers must be observant and speak regularly with the members, so they can catch any gaps in services that don't meet the members' expectations. With web-based communication, members can easily communicate and interact with the club to stay updated on statements, tee times, upcoming events, and more. This helps general managers identify any of the members' needs and concerns, and to forge a community bond, which enhances the club's value.

Then there's self-image congruence, which helps explain that people often prefer certain products or brands because they feel they fit the image they have of themselves or who they want to be. Image congruence functions as a forerunner of satisfaction and has an incidental effect on loyalty. That's understandable when you consider that a country club runs on membership and social status is one of the chief reasons for joining a private club. One of the main reasons people are motivated to join country clubs is to meet and interact with others who share common social interests. A key difference between private country clubs and other facilities is exclusivity. Country clubs are restrictive, for members and their guests only. So, the golf courses and amenities they offer are at a higher level and less crowded than public ones.

After all, besides annual membership dues, initiation fees, as high as $750,000 at some clubs, are required for admittance. In fact, membership at most clubs used to be by invitation only. Also, there is a tight screening process and anyone who doesn't meet the club's criteria can't get in. The meticulous membership application process is indispensable to ensuring elite club service and the emotional attachment—the sense of belonging and value that members have.

To position their clubs with image congruence, general managers should first figure out what the typical image congruence of their members is and the social and ideal social images. So, they can find the gap between the current image congruence and the target image congruence that the general manager of the club sets. This way they'll know what specific combination of marketing will fill the gap. Therefore, both value and image congruence are significant indicators of member satisfaction and, indirectly, member loyalty.

Involvement

Studies have established that participation has a positive effect on member satisfaction in the hospitality industry.

Also, individual involvement reflects the extent that people are devoted to an activity or related product. There is an irrefutable bond between involvement and service, quality, satisfaction, and value. Typically, consumers make decisions on repurchasing based on service quality mediated by value, satisfaction, and participation. Active members use the club facilities for golf, events, dining, tennis, fitness, swimming, and so on. Some members get involved by serving on committees that affect club decisions. People who are active and involved in the club tend to also be loyal, long-term members.

Retention

Retaining members is more important than attracting new members, because a robust membership base is the foundation for recruitment. The best source of recruiting new members is usually through a Friends and Family Program with existing members. So, when they have outstanding experiences, they will share their personal experiences and satisfaction with colleagues, friends, and family, who sometimes join the club due to that word-of-mouth endorsement.

I always try to operate with the motto that retaining members takes less effort and doesn't cost as much as recruiting new ones.

Here are some proven tips to help your club boost retention rates and ensure a high level of member satisfaction:

- Club leaders must ensure that they and their entire staff deliver friendly, best-in-class service to all members, so they feel valued, welcomed, and involved. Make the extra effort to get acquainted with their individual habits as well as their likes and dislikes to provide a personalized experience that goes beyond standard service. Everyone likes to feel important, so give it your best efforts.

- Hire the best of the best. Employees are the club's most important investment in creating and boosting membership satisfaction. I have always thought of employees as our first and best customers. Treat them fairly, with respect, and never stop encouraging their growth and development. Stand up for them, whenever the opportunity arises. The staff should operate as a well-organized team, devoted to the club's high standards and the pursuit of excellence. Remember, a happy staff equals happy members.
- Maintain a strong focus on a combination of excellence and leading edge when it comes to the amenities you offer, as well as the state of your facilities.
- Monitor national trends along with member usage patterns to steer your scheduling, programming, and master planning.
- Look at the big picture, foster a well-defined identity, and support it with structure and practices over time. Base every decision you make for the club on common goals, as well as what your club stands for and what it's all about.
- To empower members to engage in as many daily activities and special events as possible, encourage all of them to subscribe to club newsletters, email lists, the club's Facebook or LinkedIn groups, and so on. Also, the club needs to ensure accessibility and timely updates to these platforms. Research has found that there is a strong link between member satisfaction and member usage of the club.
- Provide a member area on your website to display bylaws, events, member profiles, directories, and any other pertinent or vital information.

- Encourage input from the members, be attentive to their concerns and needs and respond promptly to their comments and suggestions.

Another way to drive member satisfaction and engagement is to demonstrate that your club is open to change—request feedback to empower your members to establish their expectations. Choose a devoted group of members to conduct a satisfaction survey to keep abreast of what is or isn't working for the membership. Hand out or email the survey to the members so they can complete it at their convenience. Maintain strict confidentiality when discussing and evaluating the results. Then initiate an action plan that builds on what the members want and stops or changes what they don't want. This is important because it is very damaging for any organization to continue doing what is not popular. Believe it or not, having the ability to know when to pivot into something new, when things are not working, is a very desirable leadership trait. Set a time frame for implementing these improvements.

I tried an idea this year called "Cocktails with Frank," where I invite twelve members on a rotation basis, every other Wednesday from 6:00 to 7:00 pm (strategically before dinner), for good conversation and constructive feedback. I make it clear at the beginning of each session that this exercise is not a complaint hour but an opportunity for us to get to know one another and discuss the club affairs as if we all owned the business. No personal agenda is ever discussed, and all ideas must benefit the membership. I was amazed at how positive this get together was. Not only did I get to directly interact with the members, but I also had the opportunity to crush any rumors and increase dinner attendance on what was considered a slow night.

Membership Satisfaction Surveys

By regularly asking members for their comments and feedback, you're empowering them to help create an ideal club experience and showing them you're open to change. A survey is a great way to find out how satisfied your members are. Gather the membership committee together, or a few unbiased and dedicated members, to conduct the survey. Tell the members about the survey and that it's important they all participate.

The main point is to discover what the customers like about the club, what they don't like, and what they want more of. So, don't hold back—ask the tough questions. Welcome all feedback, negative and positive, because it all represents a great opportunity to enhance your club and be even more successful.

Here are some suggestions for the types of questions you might want to include in your satisfaction survey:

1 - How long have you been a member?

2 - Do you serve on any committees, sub-committees, or task forces?

which one(s)?

3 - Have you ever volunteered at the club?

If not, what would get you interested in doing so?

4 - Do you read our communication letters?

5 - Do you follow us on social media?

If so, is it: on:

   a.   Facebook

   b.   Twitter

   c.   LinkedIn

   d.   Instagram

6 - What changes or additions would you like in our communication tools?

7 - Have you attended any of our events in the past year?

   If so, which ones?

8 - How many rounds of golf have you played at the club in the past year?

9 - How many times do you eat at the club each month?

10 - Which events do you like the best?

11 - What kind of events would you like us to host in the future?

12 - What industry-related topics are of most interest to you right now?

13 - Do you prefer that we contact you by email, social media, or newsletters?

14 - What do you like the most about our club?

15 - What do you dislike the most about the club?

16 - What other amenities would you like the club to provide?

17 - Overall, are you pleased with the club?

18 - Would you recommend the club to your family and best friends?

19 - Do you feel the club is a good value for what you pay in dues and fees?

20 - Do you plan on renewing your membership?

Consider using an online survey tool. They're convenient, usually free or at least inexpensive, and helpful in managing the data. A print version is a great option as well.

Also, set some time during a club meeting to discuss member satisfaction. Keep the conversation fun and use some of the meeting time for members to take the survey. Another option is to hand it out or email it to members, so they'll have more time to finish it. Emphasize that all responses are confidential and are only used to improve the club for both current and prospective members.

When all the surveys are in, the dedicated group or membership committee will review and analyze the results. Underline the need for confidentiality and to respect all viewpoints. Then, present and discuss the survey results, giving all the members time to ask questions.

The next step is to draw up an action plan. Set up a forum for members to share ideas on how to best address the findings. Then, create an action plan and a timeframe for carrying out the changes.

For the final step, set the plan in action and involve as many members as you can in the process, so they're invested in enriching the club experience.

As you can see, when members are pleased with the club and see value in it, they tell others in the community, which cultivates its growth and success. It's beneficial to ensure that members are happy and actively involved from the moment they join your club. After all, it's better to invest in member satisfaction from the get-go, than to be left playing catch-up at the end.

Golden Key # 8:

Be a Master of Game Theory

It's vital to know who your members are, how to catch the interest of potential members, what they do and don't like, your competition, and what they offer. This knowledge influences your choices and leads to developing an effective business strategy, which is essential to successfully running a country club, or any other business for that matter. Game theory is a mathematical theory of strategies for increasing wins and reducing losses within prescribed constraints. It can empower clubs and hospitality businesses to predict outcomes and acquire a strategic advantage. Game theory defines logical strategy while providing a means and method to understand strategic situations you'll encounter as you work in the hospitality business. You can apply game theory when negotiating, to anticipate what trade partners and competitors might do next, so you can make the best move. It's also beneficial in preparing for future changes in the market.

First, you need to understand the game. For instance, the other club wants more members and more profit than you, and your club wants more members and more profit than them—that's the game you're playing. It starts with a set of players—the decision makers in the situation. With strategic decision making, the clubs (the players) assess both positive and negative payoffs for any move they make. And, each club tries to predict what the other club is going to do to get more members. Both clubs consider their choices, plus the payoff for the other club, while keeping their own strategy in mind. The clubs look at the specific actions available and choose the one that best fits their goal. Both clubs fit the term *rational players* because they're trying to recruit the most members and get the most profits. Both clubs can be called *intelligent players*, as each knows the other one is also trying to attain new members and get the most profits.

Businesses and others have used game theory for over seventy years. Clubs that use this process before making future decisions might gain substantial strategic sway and a notable payoff of a lot more members and profits.

Basically, it's a simple three-step method:

1. Presumptions
2. Math
3. Conclusion

We use these steps daily, but game theory goes further by ensuring our conclusions are clearly drawn from the presumptions. Typically, correct presumptions equal accurate conclusions, while incorrect presumptions add up to preposterous conclusions.

In a hospitality setting, you must have insight into your competition and a knack for anticipating how your competitors, members, and staff will react to a specific decision. You'll face various strategic choices, which directly impact your ability to achieve the desired outcome—the payoff, whether it's to increase revenue, outdo the competition, reduce risk to your club, or gain more members. To gain a strategic advantage, you must think through several variables before acting. These variables might be how your competition draws in members, their annual revenue, their place in the market, the amenities they offer, how their members rate them, or how they price their membership.

Let's look at three core strategy situations where game theory can be applied to attract more members. Every club has the tough task of pricing membership dues and considering raising them, lowering them, keeping them the same, or streamlining the fees by offering alternatives, like memberships with lower initiation fees, discounting dues to members who refer a friend who becomes a member, and so on.

You can employ game theory to estimate different outcomes for two competitive clubs. Your payoff or outcome depends on your competitor's actions. If both clubs come to an agreement to set the same membership fee, they'll bring in similar profits. But if one club sets their membership dues lower than the other club, they'll draw members away from their competitor and amplify their bottom line. If both undercut each other in membership dues, then both will end up with shrinking profits.

Game theory favors cooperation from both clubs for the best long-term outcome, but in a competitive business environment, this doesn't always happen.

If both clubs set the same high membership fees, they will mutually gain profits. If your club lowers your membership fees but the other club doesn't, you'll have a huge increase in profits for a while. When the other clubs realize what you've done, they'll lower their membership dues. Sometimes it could be too late for them. They must catch up quickly or there will come a time when they can no longer afford to lower their dues because of the amenities they are committed to. I had experienced this exact phenomenon when I was at the Middle Bay Country Club on the south shore of Long Island, NY. The club president, executive committee and I, would meet weekly to discuss these exact strategies. During my tenure at Middle Bay CC, we were the most successful out of the other competing clubs in the neighborhood.

The other clubs did not understand that it would behoove us all to work together. Lack of communication with our competitors was clearly the wrong outcome for them. If we had cooperated, perhaps we would have had better results together. Oh, well!

The game theory works similarly when applied to marketing. Clubs must choose to either spend more, less, or the same on advertising, depending on what their budget will allow and on what the other club is doing.

For example:

The Same: Both clubs might decide to pay a search engine more for increased visibility in their area. The outcome would be that both clubs would bring in more new members.

More: One club might pay even more money to ensure they would appear much higher than the other club in the search results for their area. That club would draw in a lot of new members, some who otherwise would have normally joined the competitor's club instead.

None: However, if both clubs just used the basic search engine listing, neither would gain members.

You can also use game theory to determine if making renovations and enhancements to your club is worth it to attract potential members and increase satisfaction among your current membership base. First, the club needs to see what they can afford and try to figure out if it's likely that their competitor will revamp their facilities, which would include considering the measure of standard at the other club, what they offer, the costs involved, and how pleased their members are. By raising the bar or adding new services like a spa or gym, you could outdo the other club entirely, which would merit an increase in your membership fees over what the competitive club charges. Other possibilities are that the competing club could then make renovations that meet your new improvements to level the playing field, or even ones that exceed yours and raise the standards once more.

Noncooperative

Now that you understand how you can strategically use game theory in your hospitality business, let's delve a little deeper into game theory. The two major divisions are cooperative and noncooperative. It's crucial to appreciate the ways these divisions deviate, since each one is formed from different ideas and has different uses. Often when businesspeople grow exasperated with game theory or believe it doesn't work for them, it's because they're trying to resolve the problems undertaken by one division with ideas from the other.

Noncooperative is the most common and it rose from the two principles below:

1. In business, we not only interact with a sizeable growing market but also a few other players whose tactical choices directly shape the payoffs we bring about.
2. Our choices not only impact the outcome of what we do in the present market, but are also capable of shaping the type of market we're in.

Most users of game theory are noncooperative, since each player is choosing the strategy that will benefit them individually. The players don't have any two-way agreement that will help them collectively increase their gains. Noncooperative games typically use payoff tables that list what each player will get, depending on the strategy that player uses and the tactics the other players employ. Noncooperative game theory is utilized a lot in creating online interfaces like auctions and to help align business incentives with business interests.

Nash Equilibrium, named after the famous mathematician and its inventor, John Nash, is a key for players to mathematically and logically create the best outcomes for themselves. Playing the game out move by move gets you to a result you wouldn't choose if you could make a cooperative deal. So, it's when none of the players want to change their move. A game can have one Nash Equilibrium or none at all or even several. Since Dr. Nash wrote his groundbreaking papers, lots of people have analyzed the kind of noncooperative games that end in one or more Nash Equilibrium. The economist, John Harsany, who won the 1994 Nobel Memorial Prize in Economic Sciences with John Nash and Reinhard Selten, expanded on the theory of Nash Equilibrium to include games where players don't know much about the other players' preferences. The economist, Reinhard Selten showed that Nash Equilibrium could occur in games played over time by choosing outcomes that are more sensible than others.

An example of a simple, popular noncooperative game is Rock-Paper-Scissors. A sister and brother are playing, and the boy is positive rock is the best way to go. He won't even consider any other option. His sister is sure paper is the way to go because she knows her brother likes rocks and smashing stuff with rocks, so her move is paper.

Prisoner's Dilemma

The best known noncooperative game is the prisoner's dilemma. Two partners in crime, let's say Butch and Sundance, rob a train together and now they've been arrested. You're Butch Cassidy and you're being interrogated by Marshall Wyatt Earp, but there's no way you're going to snitch on the Sundance Kid. Then, Wyatt Earp offers you a deal. All you have to do is confess to the train robbery and snitch that Sundance was also part of it, and the law will go easy on you. At the same time, unknown to you, Marshal Virgil Earp, Wyatt's brother, is in another room offering the same deal to Sundance if he will confess to the train robbery and snitch on you. You can both make a move where neither of you snitches. The outcome is you both get three years in prison. If Butch makes the move to snitch and Sundance doesn't, then he gets nine years in jail and Butch goes free. If Butch and Sundance both snitch, they both get six years in the pen.

Replace all the instances of confessing and snitching with the word *compete*. The joint payoff here is the negative sum of the total time you both spend in jail. If Butch and Sundance both snitch on (compete with) the other one, the joint payoff is -6. But they'll only spend a short time in jail if neither of them confesses and snitches. Also, all the instances of confess and snitch are dominant strategy—it gives each player the best payoff for each of the other player's choices. The double confession is Nash Equilibrium because neither Butch or Sundance could individually improve the outcome by using a different strategy.

Now imagine that you're Butch and Wyatt Earp is offering the same deal, but this time you know Sundance is getting the same offer from Virgil Earp and making his choice at the exact time you are—that means you have perfect information and the game is static. There's no reason for one player in the game to deviate from the compete-compete outcome—you'll always compete. Butch is making the best choice he can, taking into account Sundance's choice while Sundance's choice remains unchanged. And, Sundance is making the best choice he can, considering Butch's choice, while Butch's choice stays the same. That's Nash Equilibrium.

Prisoner's dilemma was designed to get both players to rat each other out. Without some way to change the consequences of the game, the outcome won't change. Even if they have the chance to talk to each other before they're arrested or if the game is made dynamic, where Sundance chooses first and before Butch makes his decision he finds out what Sundance is going to do, it's still compete-compete. In game playing, you just can't trust anyone, and no one can really trust you.

Game theory also includes socially efficient outcomes like Pareto or Kaldor-Hicks efficiencies. In these, the best output is the one with the highest joint payoff. But, that's not necessarily the best outcome for the individual player. I once had a boss who would go around and ask the staff, "How is everything?" When the staff member said, "It is all good," she would reply, "Come on, it can't be all good" and the staff member would reply, "Well, now that you ask like this, maybe I would do this and that." I have always wondered if she even realized that she would create this fertile ground for the staff to snitch on each other, even though they could have collaborated and helped each other out for a better outcome. In this particular case, the team work spirit was destroyed by this leader who unknowingly (I hope) created a back-stabbing culture.

Variations

Variations are when some of the details of the game are different and that impacts the outcome. The result of prisoner's dilemma will change if Butch and Sundance talk with each other and decide to not snitch (not compete), so instead they'll remain partners and help each other in the future. In game theory, this is called a repeated game. If the players care about each other, one of them might even be willing to go to jail to help the other one.

Cooperative Game Theory

Now that you understand noncooperative game theory, let's go over the other division—cooperative game theory. The two principles below rose from cooperative game theory.

1. We have the option of forging alliances with binding agreements on mutual actions and sharing profits.

2. We don't just allot existing value or create value through assets that yield a set profit. We're able to create new value at new rates of return by forming new combinations of assets.

When business leaders creating a new company are establishing a new organization made up of several businesses, it's advantageous to use cooperative game theory. The players, referred to as coalitions cooperative groups, interact and gather into groups that have different levels of worth. It helps the owners and leaders gauge which people and assets to bring into the company, which companies to take into a corporation, and which corporations they want for their alliance. Furthermore, it makes it easier to anticipate the amount of revenue they can expect these participating divisions to make. As you can see, cooperative game theory empowers companies to come up with better decisions on mergers and divestments.

For example, in prisoner's dilemma, the results will change if Butch and Sundance begin playing a cooperative game. It makes it possible for them to attain the ideal payoff. Also, if there are more than two prisoners and the different ones mandate different payoffs, the cooperative games that can be established hold even more importance.

This cooperative version is closer to real-life scenarios

than the classic prisoner's dilemma since it's less restrictive. Business negotiations are typically unconstrained, except when regulated by the government. Due to their pure ingenuity, businesspeople are persistently creating the sort of new combinations cooperative game theory focuses on. In fact, innovative theorists have investigated ways of merging cooperative and noncooperative game theory to shape strategic decisions. These novel efforts should bring clarity and accuracy to businesses as they calculate what value they can generate and what value they can accumulate.

Dominant

Another strategy is Dominant, which affords a player a higher payoff regardless of how the others play. With a solely dominant strategy, you get the best outcome no matter what the other player does. You made the right move...regardless. That's why the prisoner's dilemma game is so popular—betrayal guarantees a better result, irrespective of what the other person does.

People don't play games with strictly dominant strategies much because they're about doing only one thing. There isn't a dominant strategy in Rock-Paper-Scissors, but if one of the players wore oven gloves so they can't use scissors, leaving only rock and paper, then it would be a strictly dominant strategy. If you do paper, you can't lose. Once you have a strictly dominant strategy, it would be dumb for you to try anything else.

When both players have a strictly dominant strategy, the game only has one unique Nash Equilibrium, but there can also be non-equilibrium outcomes of the game that would be better for both players. The strategy can also be weakly dominant. In that case, no matter what the other players do, the strategy wins a payoff as high or higher than any other tactics.

Game theory won't do much for your club if you're making decisions carelessly and not evaluating the variables. But if club managers take the time and effort to know the market, the competition, and various potential outcomes, then game theory can be employed as a winning business strategy. There isn't any way to know everything, but game theory does illuminate choices and provide a path forward to the best outcome. If private club managers thoughtfully deliberate and calculate their actions, they can work out an ideal strategy that will result in a generous payoff.

Golden Key # 9:

Swim in Blue Ocean

In 2005, two insightful professors at INSEAD and co-directors of the INSEAD Blue Ocean Strategy Institute, W. Chan Kim and Renee Mauborgne, unleashed a business uprising. Their book, *Blue Ocean Strategy: How to Create Uncontested Market Space and Make Competition Irrelevant* (published by Harvard Business Review Press), bolstered companies to break out of crowded shark-infested waters. Fortified by researching 150 strategic moves made in thirty industries over the time span of a century, the pair publicized their discovery that the secret to success is the formation of blue oceans in an unchallenged market space, rather than an endless battle with competitors. These blue oceans support a spike in value for the organization, its staff, and its customers by pinning down a fresh want and longing that renders competition obsolete.

Value innovation is a crucial concept of Blue Ocean Strategy, which the authors initially brought to light in the 1997 article, "Value Innovation – The Strategic Logic of High Growth." This perspective is a concurrent quest of both differentiation and low cost, which leads to value for the business, the customers, and everyone involved. Ultimately, their business advice is to stop competing and start creating.

Kim and Mauborgne coined the buzzwords *Red Ocean* and *Blue Ocean*. Red ocean markets are teeming with shark-like rivals. A blue ocean signifies the simultaneous search for high product differentiation and low cost that make competition irrelevant. The established markets in all industries are red oceans. In a red ocean, industry boundaries are clear and acknowledged, plus the rules of competition are understood. In this ocean, businesses struggle to surpass their rivals to take a bite of a bigger piece of existing demand. They're called a red ocean because eventually, the market space becomes jam-packed, then profits and expansion are shrunk, which drives dog-eat-dog or bloody competition.

A blue ocean is totally different. It is an unidentified market of industries that haven't emerged yet, so it's rivalry-free. In a blue ocean, demand is cultivated, there is no competition to fight, so there are more than enough opportunities for both gainful and accelerated growth. In a blue ocean, the rules of the game aren't set yet. They are called a blue ocean because they offer the widespread potential to be explored in a deep, vast, and mighty market space for lucrative success.

Here is a breakdown of Red Ocean versus Blue Ocean strategy:

Red Ocean Strategy:

- Compete in an overcrowded market with existing demand
- Outrival the competition
- Cash in on existing demand
- Trade off value for lower cost
- Bring the entire organization's dealings into line with its strategic choice of either:
  1. Value—to show how much better your product is over the competition
  2. Cost—to simply lower the price so your product is cheaper than the competition's

Blue Ocean Strategy:

- Unknown industry or innovations create unchallenged market space

- Render competition inconsequential
- Generate and entice new demand
- Put a stop to the value-cost trade-off
- Bring the entire organization's dealings into line with its objective of both value and low cost.

Blue ocean strategists adopt a viewpoint that encourages them to challenge long-established beliefs and understand the false limits we inadvertently impress upon ourselves. Their outlook isn't like the market-competing tenet that controls the way many entrepreneurs and company leaders think. Blue Ocean Strategy proposes that to recreate aspects consumers will value, a company should use the Four Actions Framework to fashion a new value curve. The exercise consists of four basic questions:

- Raise: What product or service should be elevated well above the industry's standard?
- Reduce: What was the consequence of competing against other industries and can be decreased?
- Eliminate: What has the industry competed on long-term that should be eliminated?
- • Create: What should be created that the industry has never before given or made available to consumers?

This framework pushes business leaders to scrutinize each aspect of competition, to notice the presumptions they mechanically make when they're competing. So, they're able to seek blue oceans within their industries and bring about change. By applying blue ocean methodology, country clubs can offer innovative features and services to members that boost their competitive position in the marketplace by:

- Recognizing what the members value
- Creating unique offerings that fulfill that need
- Designing and cultivating an exceptional club

environment and culture
- Building a distinctive reputation through branding
- Establishing new market segments
- Modifying distribution channels
- And forging strategic alliances

Blue Ocean Strategy in Practice

Here are some blue ocean tactics for opening your eyes to opportunities where before you only saw limitations:

• Don't put up with industry conditions as official or absolute—shift them to your advantage. A blue ocean strategist doesn't allow the make-up of the industry influence his or her plan since, just as the original clubs created the current industry conditions, individual clubs can shape them too. Standard industry practices and logic can severely inhibit creativity, but blue ocean strategists perceive possibilities and potential profit that others can't see.

They realize that the original country club was a blue ocean strategy though it wasn't called that back then. In the post-Civil War era, rich, urban elite Americans wanted to copy the country house tradition of the British aristocracy, a place away from the city. However, that required lots of land for sports that were popular at the time: horse racing, fox hunting, cricket, tennis and so on. In other words, they needed more acreage than most homes on the outskirts of the city had. So, the answer was private country clubs. They sprung up outside major cities (in the country) in the 1880s. It started with J. Murray Forbes, who sent some friends of his an invitation that read, "The general idea is to have a comfortable club-house for the use of members with their families, a simple restaurant, bedrooms, bowling-alley, lawn tennis grounds, and also, to have race-meetings and, occasionally, music in the afternoon, and it is probable that a few gentlemen will club together to run a coach out every afternoon during the season, to convey members and their friends at a fixed charge."

Country clubs in the US didn't even offer golf until the early 1900s. So, you can see that industry boundaries are not fixed. They were shaped into the way they are now, and in that same way you can reshape them any way you need to. Changes are being made from club restaurants that are replacing old industry standards with craft and local products for the more savvy health-conscious diners of today, to marketing focused on women and families that centers on tennis, the fitness center , the pool, teen center, and kid activities with golf hardly mentioned at all, to previous by-invitation-only clubs now running promotions offering slashed or zero initiation fees, lower dues, trial memberships with money back guarantees, opening a round of golf to the public for a daily rate, and much more.

Don't beat the competition: make them irrelevant. Many clubs are caught in the trap of competing. They have accepted the red waters of competition as a necessity and they focus on surpassing the competition to attain a market advantage. The strange thing is that concentrating on developing a competitive advantage leads to an unimaginative rather than a creative approach to the market.

The more a club tries to target and outperform competitors, the more they look like their competitor. Though a competitive advantage is good, a strategy based on what potential members value is tons better. Blue ocean strategists don't copy their competitors, they focus on how to get to a state where they have no competition, where potential members who want what they're offering must come to them. They consider what it would take to draw in the mass of potential members even with no advertising. You want to offer something at your club that causes everyone who sees it or tries it to rave about it. Don't concentrate on what clubs are competing on, instead focus on what most nonmembers really want in a club, which is a more family-centered environment and membership dues at a price that people are willing to pay. So, add family-friendly activities, events, and facilities, and set membership fees at a more affordable price point. Here are some ideas, including those mentioned in other chapters:

- Eliminate foursome requirements on the golf courses
- Let people bring their dogs onto the golf course — to a lot of members they are part of their family
- Put a food truck by the entrance to the golf course
- Pick up kids from school in vans or busses and take them to the club for after-school activities
- Offer hiking and biking trips
- Add a climbing wall
- Transform the pool into a water park
- Add a kid center, kids' camp, teen center, babysitting area, and so on.
- Offer limited free memberships
- Break membership fees down into installments
- Use play now – pay later; for example, they can join the club in winter, but they don't have to pay until spring
- Seasonal memberships
- Open the clubhouse for a limited number of corporate and social events for non-members.
- Try creating and winning new demand rather than fighting over existing members. Exceeding members' expectations and demonstrating sensitivity to members' needs is a chief goal of any private club. Many clubs frequently use surveys to gauge how satisfied their members are. The surveys can result in finer market segmentation to identify

the members' individualized needs, in meeting those specific needs, and showing them what your club is offering that benefits them. Then again, blue ocean strategists do more than satisfy their active membership base. Targeting current members only anchors a country club to the red ocean of prevailing market space. Most clubs share a general classification of the type of person that they think is likely to fit in well in a country club and who will probably join a country club. This can inhibit clubs from grasping the broader potential of new demand that they can use to their advantage. Existing members represent a drop in the ocean, when weighed against all the nonmembers, who, owing to market-creating strategies, can become members. Fixing your chief marketing efforts on current members affixes your club in the red ocean of present market space. Instead of struggling to take a higher percentage of existing customers, blue ocean strategists know that potential members with other demands are obtainable.

- By turning to nonmembers, blue strategists begin to understand the specific reasons why many people don't want to join private clubs. Concentrating on marketing to existing members anchors your club in the red ocean, gazing at what is, instead of what could be. Go beyond. Uncover who the nonmembers in your area are, and why they haven't joined a country club. In the past, anything you wanted to do in your free time was there at the country club, everything in one place. Members went there for sports like swimming, tennis, and golf. They also dined at the club and even played a game of pool or had a few beers or drinks with friends in the bar. However, the concept of one spot for all your leisure activity doesn't interest millennials because they like variety. Also, golf and tennis are no longer that popular for most millennials. Additionally, a lot of business and social relationships are formed online now instead of at the country club, as generations did in the past. A blue ocean strategist would provide something fresh and new that would specifically interest nonmembers, so they'd consider joining a country club.

Millennials and young families want variety and country clubs can offer that by holding lots of different events such as: paint ball wars; block parties; Game Night; mixology classes; Bistro Night; Pizza Night; Sushi Night; Burger Night; Pasta Night; fish fry; a retro sock hop; tailgate barbeques; a book club with a coffee bar; Trivia Night in the bar with Happy Hour prices on drinks; Family Trivia Night; Guest Chef Night; Fantasy Football League party; Family Golf Day; movies on the driving range; movie nights at the pool; Sea Food Night; nutrition and healthy eating cooking classes; live music on the deck; Paint And Wine Night; Casino Royale Night; family tennis socials; murder mystery dinner theatre nights; a Super Bowl party; lots of ladies-only events, and more. Furthermore, notify your members of these events on your country club app. Millennials use apps, so clubs must have their own apps. Moreover, come up with some revamping ideas like beanbag chairs throughout locker rooms, and eliminating cell phone bans and dress codes—allow jeans, tee shirts, cargo pants, flip-flops — why not? Put a little bit of the country back in country club by setting aside an area of the property for a food-to-table garden for the restaurant and offer a spot where members can grow their own vegetables.

• Offer members a major hike in value and break the value-cost trade-off. Focus on what to exclude and reduce as much as on what to advance and create. Strive for low cost and to match or exceed the value of other clubs. Don't trade value for cost or cost for value—provide both. A differentiation strategy frequently amounts to nothing more than adding frills and trimming to the industry's typical approach. And as far as using a low-cost strategy, that usually means curtailing the industry's prevailing competing factors without producing anything new that stands out. Clubs with a blue ocean mindset don't pick between differentiation or low cost. They choose both. You want to make membership more affordable for potential members, especially millennials and families, but you also want to add more when it comes to ambiance and service. Upgrade on keeping the golf course beautiful, plus food, follow up, quality, design, and fun. When it comes to dropping membership or initiation fees, think about doing that in the offseason, since it won't affect your price integrity. Instead of discounting fees or dues outright, consider offsetting them by offering generous incentives for members to invite guests they think might want to join the club, as well as lucrative incentives for the guest themselves. Think about the long-term value of a new member, for example, the revenue they'll bring in over ten years of membership. Also, consider the purchases they'll make in the golf shop, and all the food and drinks they'll buy at the bar and restaurant, plus the guests they'll invite who will become members. So, offer a sizeable incentive for both the member and potential members they bring to the club.

Tools

Blue ocean strategy offers a full repertoire of analytical tools and frameworks for putting together and implementing moves created by Kim and Mauborgne. They are:

Value Innovation

This is the concurrent search for differentiation and low cost.

Strategy Canvas

This graphically captures the present strategic outlook and the prospects for the club.

Four Actions Framework

It's used to rebuild customer value elements.

Six Paths Framework

These are six simple methods to restructure market boundaries.

Pioneer-Migrator-Settler Map

This is a helpful exercise for an executive management team working toward profitable growth, to plot the club's current and planned portfolios on the Pioneer-Migrator-Settler Map.

Three Tiers of Noncustomers

1. Soon-to-be: Noncustomers who are on the edge of your market and waiting to leave.
2. Refusing: Noncustomers who intentionally choose against your market
3. Unexplored: Noncustomers who are in markets that are remote from yours.

Sequence of Creating a Blue Ocean

This assists clubs in developing a blue ocean strategy in the sequence of buyer utility, price, cost, and adoption. This helps the club build a feasible business model that will bring in profits from the blue ocean.

Buyer Utility Map

This encourages managers to look at things from a demand side. It gives them an idea of all the levers their club can pull to provide incomparable benefits to members, as well as the various experiences members can have with a product or service. It also helps the club recognize a full array of utility spaces that services or facilities can potentially fill. Its two facets are The Buyer Experience Cycle and the Utility Levers.

Blue Ocean Strategy can help a club generate value and a new market they didn't have before. It's based on the concept that market boundaries and industry structure are not givens and clubs should pursue differentiation and low cost simultaneously to open a new uncontested space and create novel demand with no competition. But there are limits to this approach.

Risks

Though the Blue Ocean Strategy, its tools, and framework present value input to the process, there is a risk of taking it too far:

- Ignoring Competition – Though creating an un-competitive market space to render the competition irrelevant is a great move, it might cause managers to ignore relevant competition that puts their clubs at risk. Most general managers believe that their country club offers one-of-a-kind amenities and services, but there may be other clubs that meet the members' same needs with alternatives or sub-stitutes.
- Drifting too Far – There is also the risk to a country club of its leaders getting so caught up in thinking outside of the square they forget their own strengths, principles, and mission and coast too far from their core attributes, risking failure.
- Reinventing the Wheel – Several Blue Ocean Strategy tools encourage a club to level themselves against the leading players in an industry. With this line of thought a club can fail to notice less

dominant but more promising, emerging players who can evolve into a challenge. An unchallenged market, a blue ocean, established on such an analysis, might already have other small fish swimming in it.

- Not Finding Any Fish – Another risk to look out for is that upon achieving a blue ocean, a business realizes that it was vacant for a reason. There might not be a market sufficiently sustainable to support the company long term. The blue ocean mindset assumes marketing success of value innovation, but not all businesses can realize this goal or control the promising blue ocean.

Golden Key # 10:

The "Pareto Principle" 80/20 Rule of Management

The 80/20 rule known as the Pareto Principle is a basic marketing philosophy. This principle came from the Italian economist and philosopher Vilfredo Pareto, who was born in 1848.

The way the legend goes is that on a sunny day in Italy, Pareto was walking through his garden, inhaling the fresh, vibrant scents. The tight clusters of the lush leaves and their tiny branches weighted down by the bright green, flat, banana-shaped peapods hanging from them caught his eye. Suddenly, a brilliant thought came to him—only 20 percent of his pea plants spawned 80 percent of the hale and hearty pea pods. He couldn't get the idea out of his head so, he reflected further on uneven distribution.

Pareto soon discovered that just 20 percent of the population—the richest people in Italy—owned 80 percent of the land. He studied industries and learned that usually, 80 percent of production came from only 20 percent of the companies. So, in 1906, Pareto coined what has become known as the 80/20 formula. He didn't know then that his theory would go on to prove accurate in numerous circumstances and practices, including business productivity.

Dr. Joseph M. Juran, whose grandson David Juran was my Statistic and Operations professor at the SC Johnson College of Business, was an industrial engineer and quality expert who preached quality management in the

1940s. He transformed the Japanese way of looking at quality management and was instrumental in helping build their economy, making them the modernized industrial leader that they are today.

Juran credited the 80/20 rule to the Italian economist and theorist by naming it the Pareto Principle. Juran carried Pareto's principle a step further by analyzing and studying the condition of products to see if the rule applied to them. This led to his findings that 20 percent of the flaws cause 80 percent of the problems in most products. Pareto's principle, or as some say Pareto's law, may not be a term everyone's heard of, but the 80/20 rule is commonly mentioned when speaking of economic inequities. Additionally, it's beneficial in prioritizing and handling work.

Basically, the 80/20 rule is a general truth about the imbalance of productivity. For example, around 20 percent of output can be credited with 80 percent of the outcome. Is the idea valid —that 20 percent of actions create most results—80 percent? It might not be an ironclad rule with a definitive ratio. However, even in the 21st century, over 100 years after Pareto first thought of this theory, it still holds weight. In fact, it seems the 80/20 principle is having a bit of a revival. It also follows suit with the modern expression — "work smarter not harder."

But most of the time we reference Pareto's principle to a certain condition or circumstance without a precise numerical analysis. A lot of times it doesn't exactly work out to an 80/20 ratio, but we approximate it to this simple metric with slipshod math. There are many instances where the percentage is different, such as 70/30, 60/40, 90/10, and so on. It really doesn't matter what the specific statistics are. What is important is that cause plus effect does not always have a one-to-one result. Some actions in work and life, in general, account for most of your results.

80/20 is a valuable and efficient tool when it comes to resolving complicated problems and conditions. It provides a broad view, so you can realize what 20 percent of actions or performances are producing the biggest results, and center on them. It streamlines problems to make it easier to make a smarter choice without requiring extra time or expense.

Overall, the proportion of inequity is incredibly accurate in ordinary situations. Here are some general business examples of the 80/20 rule:

- 80 percent of sales come from 20 percent of the customers.
- 80 percent of orders are for the same 20 percent of the product line.
- In IT work, only 20 percent of software bugs are responsible for 80 percent of software crashes.
- 20 percent of investors contribute 80 percent of the funding.
- 20 percent of sales representatives generate 80 percent of new business or new accounts.
- In science, 20 percent of scientist are responsible for 80 percent of breakthroughs and new discoveries.
- In the medical industry, 80 percent of health care spending comes from 20 percent of patients.
- In education, 80 percent of low-test performances as well as/or 80 percent of exceptional test performances come from 20 percent of the students.

So, now you get the idea. But, Vilfredo Pareto is also known for noting that humans often act more on emotions than logic, which is 100 percent true. So, we typically overlook the 80/20 in our everyday work.

Companies usually assign the most challenging accounts to the top sales representatives, rather than making the most of their skills by employing them in areas where they could generate the largest revenue. Businesses usually have their top employees handle the hardest work. However, it would be more efficient to assign them simpler tasks to accelerate productivity as their skills enable them to achieve solid results and work so much faster than the lower skilled staff.

Applying 80/20 to the Hospitality Industry

The wheels in your brain are probably turning as to how you can apply 80/20 to the hospitality industry and your club. There are many ways Pareto's principle can help you establish effective business solutions regarding club membership, personnel, and resources.

With all the responsibilities general managers have, it's vital that they're shrewd about allotting their time, energy and assets to areas of the club that are productive and profitable. In other words, they need to focus on the 20 percent of their work that is significant to the club's growth. And delegate the other 80 percent, the basically minor portion of their duties, to their staff. Time is a precious commodity to a busy general manager, so spending 80 percent of it on inconsequential tasks is a waste. However, it happens quite a lot — general managers working on tasks they should delegate to subordinates instead. I have heard people say it's like getting rid of 80 percent of your work. Of course, that's not true. It's more like devoting the same 20 percent but now added to the 80 percent—so 100 percent of your skills, energy, and time to the duties that are most productive. After all, keep in mind the popular 80/20 quote — Success is 80 percent attitude and 20 percent aptitude.

Additionally, reviews are crucial to the hospitality

industry, such as those posted at GolfAdvisor, Yelp, Trip Advisor, and so on in considering hotels, clubs, and restaurants. It's a fact that 80 percent of consumers read at least six reviews before making a reservation at an upscale restaurant or booking a hotel, and this includes members booking cottages at country clubs. By focusing on providing excellence in the 20 percent of the features that matter the most to members, guests, and diners, you'll ensure that your hospitality business gets great reviews.

Also, 20 percent of your members or staff account for 80 percent of your club's success. To make the most of this, you need to pin down and follow through with members or staff in the 20 percent that are contributing 80 percent to your club by:

- Utilizing dependable, state-of-the-art analytics not only to group members and employees by their worth, but to also figure out how to go about speaking with them individually.
- Interacting with each of the top 20 percent of members or employees to get their feedback or insights to make sure you're doing all you can to retain them and keep them happy.
- Provide personalized service to those top members. Show your appreciation by giving them a complimentary drink now and then, a golf cart, a golf book, a sleeve of balls, or anything that is low cost to the club but makes the member feel distinctive and valued. And ensure that all your staff always addresses those members by their names.

An example of a top 20 percent member might be one who works out once a week in the gym facilities, plays golf and tennis eight times a month, and dines at the restaurant and drinks at the bar eight times a month, and who also brings three business guests once a month, who also dine in the restaurant and drink in the bar. Encourage them to bring guests to the golf course a couple of times a month instead of once. And do what you can to motivate them to refer prospective members like themselves, who will be active in the club and bring a lot of guests.

Another example of when a country club might want to utilize the 80/20 principle is in the case of a club with, let's say, a membership of 500. They're facing a drastic drop in membership because seventy-five of their members didn't renew. So, the first step will be to gather information and conduct an analysis.

Here are two different approaches you can take to that. One utilizes 80/20:

1. Reach out to these members by phone, email or a personal visit to find out why they didn't renew. Enter that information in a dataset, analyze the data and reach for a conclusion
2. Divide these members into sections per key factors such as age, income, location, etc., create some sub-groups, then only reach out to ten to twenty in each sub-group. Evaluate the data to formulate a conclusion

The second choice is 80/20 because it saves time and energy over the first one and will most likely produce the same results you'd get with the other option.

80/20 Tips and Examples

Here are other 80/20 tips and examples that come to mind for clubs and other hospitality businesses:

- Since 80 percent of your club's proceeds come from 20 percent of your members, you should be passionate about exceeding the expectations of that

20 percent.

- Of all the social media marketing done for your club, 20 percent is giving you 80 percent of clicks, likes, and engagement. Once you're able to analyze which sites or types of posts are working for you, focus on those.
- 20 percent of your social media content should be self-promotional. The other 80 percent should be informative, interesting, and entertaining posts that your members or potential members will enjoy.
- When it comes to designing and adding content to your club's website, keep in mind that 80 percent of viewers only click on 20 percent of the pages. So, make sure those are the best-written pages and they really pop.
- If the club's teaching professionals help members master 20 percent of the basics of golf or tennis, the players will improve their game by 80 percent. Because the coach is looking at the big picture and specifically working with them on the areas that will have the strongest impact on their golf or tennis game.
- 80/20 can help your members when they're on the course having to make difficult decisions on what shot to take. If it's one they have successfully made 80 percent of the time, they should go for it. If not, they should choose another shot. Their game will improve because they're playing to their strengths and with more confidence.
- 20 percent of the club's marketing or recruiting efforts result in 80 percent of new members, so focus on the types of promotions that are working.
- 20 percent of your club's menu items bring in 80 percent of your sales, and 80 percent of them give you 20 percent of your sales. Analyze which are

which and give members more offerings that are like your top sellers. Remove the items that are only ordered a few times a month.

- Many club chefs follow an 80/20 rule of healthy cuisine, which is 20 percent healthier such as whole grains, vegetables, less meat and so on to satisfy the dietary preferences and expectations of 80 percent of the members.

- You may notice members ordering lean meats, fruits and vegetables, whole grain items, and water as their drink of choice. Then on the weekend, they may order a beer or cocktail or fried fish or chicken instead of the usual broiled or baked option. They are following the 80/20 dietary program—eating clean 80 percent of the time and indulging 20 percent of the time. Knowing the members' dining habits allows you to serve them better by offering items on the menu they most want when they want them, which increases member satisfaction.

- 20 percent of your wine and beverage list gives you 80 percent of your sales. So, if you're stocking expensive wine or alcohol in that 80 percent, take it off the menu and remove some of the other labels that don't sell well at your club.

- 80 percent of food costs come from 20 percent of items, which are usually types of meat, seafood, or luxury ingredients. Some examples are cream, butter, shrimp, smoked fish, lobster, rib eye, veal chops and so on. Of the top 20 most expensive food items your club purchases, have the chef and his/her entire team select an item to focus on each month, rotating down the list. They'll think up better choices regarding buying, storing, cooking, and serving it.

- Of all the facilities or amenities at the club, members use only 20 percent of them 80 percent of the time. So, do everything you can to make those features or areas even more exceptional.

- 80 percent of problems caused by members or staff come from only 20 percent of them. For the portion that's staff, you should consider retraining them. Frequently, consistent training produces results. But, if the training doesn't work for them, you might have to let them go.
- 80 percent of tardiness and absenteeism occur with only 20 percent of the staff, so find a way to reward the 80 percent for almost always showing up for work and on time.
- 80 percent of the work from the club's volunteer board of directors may come from 20 percent of the volunteers. So, be sure to recognize and reward the top percent in some way.
- When a club's general manager is assessing the mid-year growth toward the club's goals, 20 percent will be crucial—essential to 80 percent of the club's success. So, he/she needs to focus on those areas where they are making so much progress.
- 20 percent of your staff might be getting an 80 percent fraction of the total wages paid. Evaluate their performance to ensure that their high earnings reflect the level of work they are doing.
- 80 percent of a club's budget for building and designing the fitness area should be put toward the front get-together area and the locker room, creating a chic design that inspires members to enter and exercise.
- 20 percent of the subjects on a meeting agenda often occupy 80 percent of the time. Review that portion and try to condense it for the sake of time management and to keep attendees from getting frustrated by an overlong meeting.

- In the pro-shop where you sell golf and tennis items, 20 percent of the items generate 80 percent of the sales and conversely, 80 percent of the items generate only 20 percent of sales. So, consider dropping the low sellers and adding more items that are like your top sellers.
- 20 percent of a management team's work produces 80 percent of their success for that project. By concentrating on the 20 percent, the most important tasks, they can accomplish more. So instead of just fulfilling the requirements of the project, they're focused on executing the project in the best way possible.

Turn It On Its Head

You can also turn the 80/20 principle on its head by prioritizing the 80 percent of members who only account for 20 percent of the club's success. Here are some things to try or to keep in mind to get that 80 percent to become more active:

- Score your members from A to E.
- The As and Bs are your top 20 percent.
- Compile a cache of rewards such as having a photographer come in to take family, couple, and individual photos of members—they all get one 8 x 10 copy complimentary, movie passes, group outings, a food tasting party at the restaurant, closed-door events, special discounts and more.
- Offer these types of rewards regularly, like every quarter or so.
- Provide a lot of personal attention to your C and D members to motivate them to become more active and move up to the A and B level.

Doubts About 80/20

There are some trepidations over 80/20 when it comes

to the workforce and management. There are people who feel it does more harm than good. These concerns include:

- It discourages clubs and other organizations from drawing on the ideas, opinions, and passions of all their employees to propel the company forward.
- It initiates rivalry between workers for limited rewards, which deters teamwork and collaboration.
- Even though employees don't contribute equally to the club's success, it's irrational and unproductive to presume this is due to an arbitrary division.

The 80/20 rule is intriguing, and the pattern pops up everywhere. The key to this timeless time management principle is to prioritize. It is a valuable concept when exploring input and outcomes. It's useful with lists of things to do or goals. And, offers a helpful framework for dealing with a variety of issues. It encourages you to look at those areas that will have the biggest impact on your club.

The Pareto Principle is a reminder to not focus excessively on fixing what's wrong, but to concentrate more on leveraging what's right, because that's what your members will respond to. However, at the same time, keep in mind that 80/20 does serve a practical purpose, but 20 percent of anything, especially when it has to do with people, isn't a trivial amount.

Golden Key # 11:

Innovate or Die

Yogi Berra once said, "The future ain't what it used to be." And that was never truer than it is today.

A whirlwind of innovation is advancing, rushing us off our feet faster than we can respond.

When you hear the expression "innovate or die," companies like Radio Shack, Sears, and Toys R Us come to mind, but the saying also applies to the hospitality industry and private clubs. We need innovations our members can see and use, for example, golf carts with GPS, video, music, and interactive games. Plus, we need operational innovations such as ECRM systems that convert more prospects into members faster and easier.

Most club managers tend to avoid risks, so they don't explore innovative approaches and ideas, even though it's highly advantageous to do so. But, your club needs to be what your members want it to be, which means to meet those changing needs you must be innovative. So, come up with and spearhead inventive new ways of doing things.

Show the board you're a creative thinker. If you think of an idea, draw up a plan and present it. You never know what might stick. The management at many private clubs seems to recoil from anything different. However, state-of-the-art innovation isn't a matter of cost-benefit analysis, it's basic survival.

Sure, back in the 20th century people routinely joined the country club their parents used or became members to gain respect and close deals on the golf course, but none of those reasons appeal to millennials. And, they also don't fit the needs of the modern, busy, two-income families with children.

The effective way to cater to families is to resolve an issue for them. For example, Cheval Golf & Athletic Club in Tampa, FL, offered a solution to the problem of latchkey kids in the communities around the club. They purchased two buses and a van to pick up children from area schools daily for all types of youth athletic programs at the club. Trained counselors worked with and took care of the children, who participated in fun and healthy activities like swim meets, golf clinics, tennis matches, and so on until their parents came for them. Sometimes parents even met their kids at the tennis court or golf course, played a game or two together, then ate supper at the restaurant before they all went home for the day.

The kids were happy, playing at the club, the parents were relieved their kids were in a safe, productive after-school program, and Cheval was thrilled when their membership more than doubled, from 100 families to over 200.

Deliver top-shelf services, or your members will go somewhere else. Your innovations don't have to be high-tech, they can be as simple as attaching sensors to maintenance equipment, so course managers can tell how long it takes various employees to finish a task. Also, so the groundkeepers will know where the golf carts are, so they can work on the areas where no one's playing at the time. And your innovations don't have to be a grand production. They can be as down-to-earth as monthly sunset cookouts, dining at the 10th tee, concert on the driving range, or a petting zoo for the little ones. It just takes something that pops, that make members feel special, makes guests want to join, or makes operations easier and more productive. It's not all about a spark of genius, instead it's generated by:

Hard Work

Meticulously Reviewing and Evaluating Areas of Opportunity

The Members' Needs

"Genius is one percent inspiration and ninety-nine percent perspiration," as the great innovator Thomas Edison said.

Here are some major areas to consider innovating at your club and amazing examples of what some other country clubs have done:

Dining:

Clubs have really relaxed their dress codes in the dining area. Nowadays people want to stop by the club to eat after work. If they must go home and change first, then they simply won't come, they'll go to another restaurant. So, clubs had to get innovative and allow casual clothing, even blue jeans are permitted at most clubs now. However, chefs still prepare the menu items with great care and seriousness to provide the finest cuisine though they're introducing modern trends, including healthier veggie and vegan options, farm-to-table, entire meals that can be served up conveniently and quickly -- even taken on the road or eaten away from the club, plus more international cuisines and ethnic foods. Also, many are offering gluten-free breads, cookies, and pastries. Some have initiated chocolate tasting bars. Other popular innovations are digital tablet computers for menus, wine lists, and ordering. Many clubs are also now using mobile or wireless payment options.

Here are some innovations put in place by other clubs:

- The North Hills Club in Raleigh, NC, implemented a kids' menu attached to an Etch A Sketch®

drawing toy and family-themed nights with child care provided.

- The Detroit Athletic Club in Detroit, MI, launched a secret shopper program in the restaurant and they also got innovative with the parking lot across from the Detroit Tigers' stadium, using it as a tailgating dining venue during game time.
- The Medinah Country Club in Chicago, IL, has a chicken coop and a food truck. The chickens and fresh eggs are a symbol to members and guests that they care deeply about the quality of the food they serve. So, they have forty hens and thirty to forty beds of vegetables and herbs in their Meacham's Garden. They also have a food truck offering burgers, smoothies, street foods, and homemade snacks.
- The Old Memorial Golf Club in Tampa, FL, goes out of their way for their members at the Locker Grill, providing pretty much anything the members want for dinner, including exotic food on request such as elk or ostrich.

Also, bars are focal points of social activity and need their own place in a clubhouse, on a patio, or by a fire pit. And craft beer and craft cocktails should be added to the menu. Some even offer gourmet soft drinks. You can also host special events at the bar, like a dance competition or wine tasting that will draw in the regulars along with the members who don't come that often. You could also have a business networking event at the bar for members and potential members

Golf:

Traditional golf isn't going anywhere, but at the same time innovations such as Topgolf and digital golf games are now used in private clubs. Here are some other golf innovations:

- Some clubs have a Swing Robot or another type of robotic swing trainer. It's a great tool to teach members to change their motion so they can develop a proper swing. In as little as three weeks of practice with Swing Robot, members can develop a successful swing.

- Golf Boards are used on courses at Blackrock in Hingham, MA, Westin Kierland Resort & Spa in Scottsdale, AZ, and more than 500 other courses across the US. Instead of walking or using a cart, the members set their golf clubs on the front of these motorized skateboards, step on, and take off. It's a lot like surfing, snowboarding, or skateboarding. Golf Boards add an extra element of fun for players, make rounds faster, and cause less wear to the course than carts do.

- At the Empire Ranch Golf Club in Folsom, CA, golf coach Will Robins guarantees golfers a ten-stroke improvement over their baseline average. His inventive training approach consists of ten sessions for twelve weeks with teams of six golfers. Half the sessions are on the course, the other half are on the driving range or at the short-game practice area. Golf coaches at Empire Ranch continually push the power and responsibility onto the student. To start the process, the coach and golfer identify areas for improvement and set goals, then the student signs an agreement promising to show up on time. This type of coaching utilizes playing lessons as tee sheet feeders. An on-course playing lesson can be added on a stand-alone basis at any time.

- At Magnolia Plantation Golf Club in Lake Mary, FL, the Mike Bender Golf Academy uses an innovative stone target wedge range for short-game effectiveness and uniqueness. At the hard-target wedge range, members hit striped balls at concrete target slabs. Also, the Ridgewood Country Club in Paramus, NJ, uses a hard-target wedge range. At both learning centers, members enjoy building accuracy and distance control on pitch shots. At Ridgewood, a special 12-foot-by-80-foot concrete hitting station was also installed, padded, and then overlaid with new synthetic turf.

- OpenRounds' founder, Jonathan Wyeth, has developed "reciprocal golf," somewhat like Priceline but for golf. With OpenRounds, a country club can help its members gain access to clubs in other cities and states. If you live in Chicago, your club can set up a round at a club in Miami when you travel there for business or for a vacation. It's an additional benefit for members and the course they visit earns extra revenue from that round. For every round of golf the clubs in the network sell to visiting guests, OpenRounds earns a 20 percent commission.

- Shanty Creek Resort in Bellaire, MI, the Largo Golf Course, outside St. Petersburg, FL, and the Haggin Oaks Golf Course complex in Sacramento, CA, all offer FootGolf. In this innovative game, soccer balls replace golf balls on a regular course with 21-inch diameter cups. Also, the rules are so close to golf that both games can be played simultaneously by two different groups. And interest is growing for this bold game that blends soccer and golf.

Club Facilities:

Clubs are remodeling their facilities to deliver the total year-round experience members want. Many of the new designs cater to the members' professional needs with conference and business centers, plus meeting halls. Country clubs are also building family-friendly playgrounds, day care centers, and water parks. Clubs are trying innovations like rebuilding their pools—

doubling the size to wow the kids or favoring the grownups with resort-style pools complete with swim-up bars.

- The Club at Bella Collina in Montverde, FL, transports their members to a fantasy atmosphere. The locker rooms look like Roman baths and include saunas and hot tubs. The dining area overlooks picturesque courtyards. Also, cobblestone paths and vine canopies connect a series of buildings.
- Additionally, the Midland Country Club in Michigan replaced the traditional pool with an aquatics center that emulates Disney water parks. Plus, they added a daycare area and a new fitness center. They also put in indoor simulators, so members can play in winter with friends and family or just use a timer.
- Many clubs have also made innovations to their golf courses.
- The Monarch Bay Golf Club in San Leandro, CA, was redesigned into a breathtaking scenic course with seaside links.
- The Tarpon Woods Goff Club in Palm Harbor is a certified Purple Heart course, remodeled to cater to wounded warriors. They even sculpted the bunkers on the course to make them easier for veterans with prosthetics to access.

Operations:

Expectations have changed radically. Members are now searching for value in their club investment. There are many novel ways to market the club to prospective members. Some new concepts private clubs are adopting are:

- One-day or one-month memberships so guests can see the club.

- Play for free programs, so non-members can be a member for the day at no cost if they bring three non-members to play golf at the course for a discounted guest fee.
- And, at the Pinnacle Peak Country Club in Arizona, for a fully refundable deposit, nonmembers between ages thirty-five and forty-five get a one-year trial membership before committing to an initiation fee. Monthly dues are lowered by 75 percent.
- At the Ridgemont Country Club in Rochester, NY, they offer economic partial memberships that, though they have restrictions, have greatly accelerated their membership base.
- Jim Singerling, former CEO of the Club Managers Association of America, came up with an innovation for insurance. Since premiums were so expensive, many clubs had trouble paying them. He presented the case to the insurance companies that underwriting benchmarks for clubs over-assess the risk. At the same time, CMAA established the ClubDNA Program to leverage the association's membership for lower-cost coverage. Clubs boosted the value of coverage while reducing their premiums. Clubs can use the money they save to make improvements for their members.
- The Brandermill Country Club in Midlothian, VA, needed funds to completely refurbish their pool. They utilized crowdfunding offering club members:

Ten guest green fees valid for $500, including cart, plus another ten free.

A brick with their family, children, or company name on it for a $300, or three bricks for just $500.

Corporate packages for a personalized brick, plus a twenty-player golf outing, were available for $1,000.

100 pool-only memberships for $995, which members sold to friends, neighbors, and colleagues. There were incentives for selling them.

And they held a "Cocktails For a Cause" tournament that included an auction with a broad spectrum of interesting offerings to bid on.

Technology

Members typically now use their cells for other reasons than phone calls while at the club: texting, apps, Internet searches, etc. Also, it's now common for members to make online payments to the club, access their membership accounts online, and make online reservations for tee times and dining. Not long ago, using cell phones on the court or making reservations online were big innovations.

Since technology is now utilized at the clubs, there have been many other innovations, including:

- FAIRWAYiQ software efficiently helps with maintaining golf courses. They install a wireless base station, attach wireless sensors to carts and other equipment, so at any time they know exactly where everything is, which stops backups caused by slow foursomes.
- GreenSight Agronomics leases small flying drones with infrared cameras to create a detailed map of the golf course. That live data helps clubs manage the course. The Federal Aviation Administration allows GreenSight's drones to fly outside of a human operator's line of sight, so they can cover large areas.

Managing Innovation

Innovation has to do with generating value, not necessarily technology or new inventions. Innovation is quickly transforming our lives. We must accept that it is and will continue to influence the club environment. Also, it's an effective, strategic management tool. We need to not only generate new ideas but also initiate a plan to manage those ideas.

New ideas must be presented, then evaluated so we can choose the best ones. Then we can examine those ideas to assess the right balance between their offerings for the young generation and the older one in a constantly changing environment. And at that time, though we can't be fully sure of the risk compared to the return linked to each innovation, we need to move forward. More general managers need to inspire innovation, form strategic innovation teams, and encourage club cultures in which innovation can thrive.

It's essential that club management and their boards study and fully understand the process of innovation and how to apply it to both the tangible and intangible. Tangible elements of innovation specify a vision for the future, the end goal you're working toward. However, an example of an intangible element would be the culture of the club that the innovations must align with.

Club management should consider:

Are you leaders or followers?

Are you willing to embrace the future or are you content with the status quo?

Innovation involves making a club superior and distinctive as well as happy and relaxing. It's about inclusion, offering a great club experience for men, women, and their children. It's a place of social gatherings and making friends—a place where everybody knows your name.

We must take new and innovative steps to make our

private clubs more appealing to members and potential members. The overall club experience needs to exceed the expectations of the members. And these are the clubs that will move into the future.

Golden Key # 12:

Every CEO Should Have A Coach

Along with the Board of Directors, the General Manager (some clubs use the title CEO, COO Managing Director, or President) determines the private club's goals, values, mission, and standards. So, CEOs define the entire culture of the club. Therefore, private clubs, hotels, restaurants, and other hospitality businesses have characteristics and attitudes, both positive and negative, that trickle all the way down from the top.

The Modern CEO

US country clubs have been around for over 130 years—since the 1880s, but today's CEOs are under more pressure and face more challenges than any in the past. They are accountable for: board, committee, and member relations and responsiveness; carrying out the club's vision and mission; visibility; marketing; leadership; administration; team building; communication; club culture; member services; serving as a role model; maintenance; owned and leased equipment and service contracts; sports; the kitchen; amenities; dining and beverage services; special event and social planning; HR and legal issues; employee retention and training; multi-department staff hiring; solid financial stewardship; annual and long-term budgets; capital and future capital planning; upon all of which the success or failure of the club rests. Additionally, they handle these crucial multifaceted responsibilities while dealing with rapidly fluctuating markets, technologies, and workforces, and they do it all under amplified fiscal and legal scrutiny.

Moreover, CEOs typically have a sixty- to eighty-hour work week during busy periods. Along with the demanding workload and putting out fires, general managers frequently must pacify a small percentage of tactless or discourteous members who repeatedly complain about the club, amenities, the board, club rules, club fees, club dues, club events, club employees, even other members—without validation. I would never forget the time when I had to deal with a forty-five-year-old legacy member (meaning his parents were members as well) who practically grew up at the club and made sexual advances to a fifteen-year-old staff member at the snack bar. Yes, those creeps belong to private country clubs too. We had to file charges with the grievance committee that made the recommendation to the board to have him expelled. The key here is to follow the process and always do what is right regardless of political fallout.

They must be exceptionally diplomatic to deal with inner politics and a lot of second guessing from members. There is also the constant challenge of having enough workers to meet member expectations while adhering to budget restrictions. They're faced with a continuous stream of critical issues to tackle and solve. CEOs must multitask, be energetic, attentive, and constantly aware of the staff, the club, the board, the members, and the competition to be successful. Also, they are the one and only decision maker on tough choices, many times for departments they may not even have enough real-time performance information on.

This type of stress can cause anxiety, panic, and physical ailments, which powerful leaders don't like to disclose. Many CEOs fear if they reveal the level of stress they're under, others will think they are not capable of doing their job or that they won't last much longer in that job. CEOs who believe they can deal with all of it by themselves are likely to burn out, and become mentally exhausted or depressed, which leads to them making poor decisions or no decisions.

Though a CEO might have made countless strong, solid decisions for years, it only takes one bad decision to tumble from the lofty heights. The truth is that in the ruthless business world of the 21st century, CEOs are only as good as their last decision, and their knack for keeping ahead of the competition. Coaches center on goals and priorities to help the CEO make emboldened choices they might not have made otherwise. A coach helps to substantially boost the available options, so the CEO makes significantly better decisions.

However, many powerful business leaders don't think they need anyone's advice. Though all exalted professional athletes, musicians, actors, and so on have coaches, a lot of chief executive officers and general managers are often skeptical of coaching. Even nowadays, among some club CEOs there's a stigma attached to coaching. A residue of that old-fashioned idea that coaching is remedial still exists. Coaching is usually prompted from the standard subject of growth presented in a CEO's evaluation as an equal, joint decision of the CEO and the board, since, typically, both sides agree on coaching before it takes place. Boards should have a modern take on and understanding of high-performance coaching. If a board is pro-coaching, it helps secure the CEO's success.

But coaching has a stigma attached to it for many board members, especially those raised in an era when coaching was used as a type of corrective measure that a CEO would never take on voluntarily. But instead of a remedial step, coaching is a strategic move to advance to a higher level of performance. Wanting a coach or advisor isn't an indication of an underlying ineptitude or deficiency, rather it's a key attribute of a superior leader. Coaching has to do with advancing from admirable to remarkable. It hones and builds up a leader's capabilities. Coaching can make someone who is great, greater. No Olympic athlete would ever think of not using a coach. Not only Olympians but all elite athletes have one.

So, CEOs should see taking on a coach as a sound decision, a tool for refining and even surpassing their already top-level, overachieving performance. Also, when a CEO seeks out a coach, it proves their commitment to personal improvement and establishes a notable example for all personnel to follow. It shows that the CEO is anxious to grow and advance for the good of the club. Club board members should realize that CEO coaching is often the difference between a good organization and an amazing one.

Coaches offer the CEO a chance to reflect and find his/her own way. The coach knows the CEO is the expert. They're there to draw that knowledge out of the CEO so they can grow. They guide the CEO in exposing traits that are already within them— the ones they need to do their absolute best. CEOs of clubs need coaches with a good grip on best practices related to the private club industry. The coach should offer an impartial view on the choices the CEO makes and their interpersonal skills as they interact with others. The coach must be perceptive, highly intelligent, neutral in their evaluation, and personalize the coaching to the CEO's specific needs. Effective coaches never make a client feel inferior or lacking, instead, they get the CEO excited about attempting something new or in a different way.

Coaching is personal and confidential, between the coach and the CEO. But bankruptcy, loss of top managers, unbecoming press coverage, and other events can occur, which bring the CEO to take ownership of the situation and to acknowledge that they're working on their management style or whatever short-coming might have contributed to the problem. It's done with an open, honest attitude of full discourse, with nothing to hide. Such a message can have a positive impact on the club and on the CEO's reputation.

Unchecked Egos

CEOs experience status and incentives close to those of a celebrity. Which is part of the reason the chief causes of CEOs failing don't have anything to do with expertise, competency, or experience. Instead it's due to arrogance, ego, and out-of-date leadership styles.

Many CEOs have bad habits stemming from unconstrained egos. Powerful leaders have high self-esteem, but unfortunately for many, the higher their self-confidence the less liable they're open to the advice or opinions of others. As many as 82 percent of new CEOs flounder because they dropped the ball when it came to forging partnerships with their staff and associates. Self-centeredness and lack of emotional intelligence contribute to the failures of many CEOs, as does imposter syndrome. There are a surprising number of CEOs with imposter syndrome, who are afraid that they're horrible at heading the company. Unlike their staff, they own or basically own the place, so resigning is not a realistic option. They have to look deeper to uncover a further sense of significance and importance in their work and fresh ways to re-engage.

Additionally, greater power often makes people even more egotistical. Studies have revealed that leaders who possess a high level of authority usually dispose, reject, or misconstrue other people's opinions. Appreciating and dealing well with others' views is essential to effective leadership. That ability—empathy—comes from self-awareness. When a person of high power is given even more authority, it lowers their capacity for feeling empathy and compassion. Essentially, having power and control impacts the mirror system of the brain where we're wired for understanding what other people are feeling or going through. Researchers discovered that even a minor amount of power shuts down that function of the brain and the skill to empathize with others.

Empathy and self-awareness are the merits of a mature, developed mind. People who are not easily affected by stress and can manage internal conflicts have an interconnection with other people and a healthy, happy outlook. CEOs with minds that stimulate expansive perspectives can perceive the problems and erratic challenges confronting them. So, when a CEO doesn't have these crucial traits, when they're emotionally detached, unaware of their own personal motives, they're ineffective as leaders. A CEO's inability to relate well to other people causes conflicts between them and their management team as well as board members. From time to time we've all heard news stories about things like this happening — of some CEO of a huge corporation having to resign or get fired.

However, with a conscious effort, these abilities that are vital to effective top-level leadership can be cultivated. When a CEO or anyone knows themselves, objectives are clearer and it's easier for them to understand others' views, goals, principles, and character traits.

With coaching, a CEO can transform the club's culture in several ways. They change it from:

- Putting out fires to crafting maintainable procedures that work every time.
- Controlled communication with no feedback to fostering a supportive environment of risk taking
- Finding faults and failings to acknowledging and

elevating the staff for their strengths

- The CEO managing all problems themselves to the CEO supporting their staff to prevent and work out problems
- The CEO functioning as the only one who can endorse anything to championing collaboration and resolution

By coaching CEOs to acknowledge and use each team member's strongest attributes in implementing the club's vision, the coach leads the CEO to achieve their targeted goals. Also, when the CEO takes a lesson from their own coaching to inspire, coach, and transition others into top leaders, the CEO can structure a communal environment where team members work more efficiently, both together and on their own.

Coaching also helps CEOs handle conflict successfully. Usually, some staff or members are satisfied, even pleased, with a specific decision by the CEO, while others are dissatisfied with it. Pretty much everything that crosses the CEO's desk makes some personnel and members happy and some unhappy (80/20). A coach's support helps CEOs maintain the balancing act needed to walk that thin line. Conflict management is so vital to an organization that if a CEO ignores conflict, a domino effect begins:

- They don't make decisions
- Other employees follow suit, becoming unproductive
- The initial problems the CEO wouldn't make decisions on get worse
- The entire organization winds down

A CEO who succeeds in handling conflict in a positive way gets to the core issue, and with objectivity makes the decision that will result in the best overall outcome for the club. This is a crucial skill that empowers the entire organization.

Coaches also work on communication skills, so CEOs can present their message and their ideas with certainty in a way that is easy to understand and has an impact. CEOs also increase productivity by working with a coach, and that fosters a dynamic club culture, which heightens the club's overall performance and productivity.

In addition, coaching helps CEOs gain clarity and develop strategies to diminish distractions and focus on actions in line with the club's values, vision, and mission. Coaches inspire CEOs to pursue projects that drive them forward, so they discover novel, innovative techniques and maintain pace with the modern market. With a proficient coach, a CEO will boost their leadership skills.

So, coaching is clearly beneficial, and the growth and profitability it generates more than compensates for the initial investment.

Self-Awareness is Critical

Self-awareness and the evolution it boosts, pooled with a professional viewpoint and practices, are the core of great coaching. From a CEO's inner reflection on their motives, ideals, and character traits, they can build an infrastructure of successful leadership, vision and behavior with that heightened self-awareness as the foundation. That was never truer than in today's rapidly changing environment.

To do that, CEOs need to hear the truth about bad moves they make or their flaws, but no one will tell them. However, they're the one everyone points to when something goes wrong. Not using a coach is like saying, "I'm always right." But, effective CEOs realize they don't know it all. They assemble an intelligent staff who have expertise in the areas that they don't, and they appreciate the knowledge their employees bring to the table, as well as the opportunity to learn from them. Because they believe in their own professional development, they encourage and support their staff's development as well.

Being a CEO is a lonely job. Board members are highly useful to a CEO, but they're not the best ones to speak to about their doubts and worries. There are some things a CEO just can't discuss with the board, and some things they can't discuss with their leadership team. A CEO needs a cohort of sorts that they can speak freely with— someone who is honest, impartial, perceptive, and respectful.

Often leaders see themselves one way while their staff sees them another way. This lack of self-awareness can hinder a CEO's career. The bigger the gap, the more the leader resists change. These blind spots CEOs have regarding themselves make it tough to fashion a club culture that encourages honesty and fairness.

Exceptional CEOs help their leadership teams attain success. They are also brave, driven, enthusiastic, courageous, truthful, and dependable. But in today's high-stress environment, leaders need a cohort of sorts who will tell them the truth about their shortcomings. The board seldom does, and their employees never will. Their staff is uncomfortable in saying anything negative to them, and many boards are not thorough in providing feedback regarding possible self-improvements the leader can make, especially if they're happy with the club's finances. But a coach can help CEOs delve into their inner and external strengths and weaknesses.

Many have never had the chance or the time for self-discovery. Coaches assist CEOs with self-exploration to remove the invisible and self-induced hurdles standing between them and their goals. Coaches help their clients identify these barriers, where they originated, where they come from, and how to knock them down. These hurdles must be eliminated for the good of the club. The result is the best leader imaginable.

Coaches offer objective opinions, free of bias. They ask the clients questions that open them up, that make them think—questions others are afraid to ask.

CEOs, like anyone, can only find self-awareness with a frank assessment of their emotional strengths and weaknesses, principles, attitudes, character traits, and unresolved issues. Just like everyone else, CEOs are whole, individual people, not just a job performance or a set of skills. Self-examination is crucial to personal and professional growth. This is especially true for CEOs, as some of them don't think they need to change anything about themselves.

Self-awareness lets CEOs increase their capacity for knowing what to pursue and what not to. With coaching, CEOs can enhance their self-awareness in several ways. Here are a few methods that CEOs have found beneficial:

- Key Turning Points—CEOs consider the crucial points in their career and personal life that molded their ideals, point of view, and conduct. They look at the professional choices and experiences that shaped their personal growth and the consequences both good and bad. Then they can discover where this awareness leads them to regaining and nurturing latent or neglected aspects of themselves.
- Exercise for Gap in Abilities—CEOs list their greatest personal strong points and character traits. Then they explain how each one's expression has become undeveloped or blocked. For each gap, they note what they need to do to expand those aptitudes and shrink the gaps in their role as a CEO and their life.
- Pinpoint Personal Vulnerabilities—CEOs, like all humans, have hidden anxieties, emotional blind

spots, and some dysfunctional behavior that can become unseen driving forces of their lives. Usually, blind spots aren't noticed when everything's good. Most CEOs center their focus inward so it's especially hard for them to see these blind spots. But these spots can be dangerous when things aren't working out so well. Most CEOs need a reality check sometime—the opinion of an unbiased coach.

Successful CEOs are tuned in to others as well as to their own passions and tactics that drive them, and their own interests, both seen and unseen. Self-awareness is the foundation of competency in both business and personal relationships. In the fast-moving hospitality industry, we rely on continuing relationships. We humans are complex, always growing and evolving. So, it takes work to build business relationships. Candid, constructive criticism from coaches helps CEOs excel in their career journey.

Even CEOs who have gained success without a coach should consider using one to establish an even stronger legacy and increase the wealth for their organization and their family. It's especially beneficial for CEOs to get started with a coach early in their career. Coaching helps CEOs focus on their most earnest aspirations and strategies, while also becoming less selfish and more aware of others.

Conclusion

Hospitality is a challenging industry, but I love it. And the 12 Golden Keys in this book will help you make the most of all the hard work you put in as a CEO or general manager, beginning with the first key—You Can't Grow As A Leader If You Don't Develop Others. One of the most important traits of winning leaders is their dedication to helping others evolve and advance by inspiring, enabling, mentoring, and training them. It's a big responsibility, but the reward of seeing your staff flourish and advance in the workplace is more than worth it.

The second key is Over-Invest In People. Your business is shaped by the people you hire. They represent your club and are the key to your success. The best clubs consider their personnel an investment instead of an expense. Over-investing in your employees can cost a pretty penny, but it will drive your club to success. It's an investment you're guaranteed to reap rewards from.

The next key, the third one, is Diversity. The hospitality industry is filled with people of different ages, races, and cultures. It's fundamental to your club's success to acclimate and empathize with people of diverse ethnicity and cultures, both members and employees. This can be done through diversity training, diversity management, and overcoming the challenges of diversity.

The forth key is Embrace Change. Country clubs need to engage in active transition and restructure their company around new processes. Change is constant in the hospitality industry and it impacts customers, managers, and employees. But, don't let paradigms or opposition to change get in the way. We live in an era of never-ending change. Employees who are flexible and can easily adapt, and managers who are skilled in leadership will pave the way to new innovations in the hospitality industry.

The next key is the fifth, which is Utilizing Social Media for Marketing. It's advantageous for all hospitality establishments, including private clubs, to embrace the power of social media platforms such as Twitter, Facebook, Instagram, Pinterest, LinkedIn, YouTube, Trip Advisor, and blogging to grow their businesses and increase profits.

The sixth key is Be A Student of the Obvious. In pursuit of answers and tactics, clubs and other hospitality businesses often dismiss what is right under their noses – the obvious. Instead of searching for complex solutions, look for simple solutions to complicated problems. Think innovation rather than creativity. Focus on doing what you're doing now, but in a more effective way.

Then we have the seventh key, which is Member Satisfaction. The club's success and reputation rest in the hands of happy and loyal longtime members who will recommend your club to their family, their friends, and others in the community, which cultivates its growth and success. Also, make sure the members are happy and actively involved from the moment they join your club. After all, it's better to invest in member satisfaction from the get-go, than to be left playing catch-up at the end.

That brings us to the eighth key, which is Be A Master of Game Theory. It can be employed as a winning business strategy to predict outcomes and acquire a strategic advantage. It defines logical strategy while providing a means and method for understanding strategic situations you'll encounter as you work in the hospitality field. It's also beneficial for preparing for future changes in the market. There isn't any way to know everything, but game theory provides a path forward to the best outcome. Private club managers can utilize game theory to work out a strategy that will result in a generous payoff.

The ninth key in the book is Swim in Blue Oceans. The idea is to stop competing and start creating. Blue Ocean Strategy can help a club generate value and a new market that wasn't there before. It's based on the concept that market boundaries and industry structure are not givens, therefore clubs should pursue differentiation and low cost simultaneously to open uncontested spaces and create new demand with no competition. The buzz words for this strategy are red ocean and blue ocean. Red ocean symbolizes the established markets, which are teeming with shark-like rivals. Blue ocean signifies the search for both high product differentiation and low cost that make competition irrelevant.

Then, we have the tenth key which is the Pareto Principle—the 80/20 Rule of Management. It's based on the general fact that productivity is unbalanced. 80/20 is a valuable and efficient tool when it comes to resolving complicated problems and situations. The principle provides a broad view, so you can realize that 20 percent of actions or performances are producing the biggest results and center on them. It streamlines problems so that it's easier to make smarter choices without requiring any extra time or expense. Overall, the proportion of inequity is incredibly accurate in ordinary circumstances. Pareto's Principle is a reminder to not focus excessively on fixing what's wrong, but to concentrate more on leveraging what's right because that's what your members will respond to.

That brings us to the eleventh key, which is Innovate or Die. If you don't move toward the future, you'll become part of the past. The hospitality industry and private clubs need innovations members can see and use, as well as operational innovations. We must take innovative steps to make private clubs more appealing to members and potential members. Clubs that offer an innovative experience that exceeds the expectations of the members are the ones that will move into the future.

At last, we're presented with the twelfth golden key, which is Every CEO Should Have A Coach. CEOs define the entire culture of the club and they are under more pressure and face more challenges today than ever before. Coaching helps CEOs focus on their most earnest aspirations and strategies, while also learning to be less selfish and more aware of others.

The knowledge I'm giving you with these twelve keys, like all learning, is power. It leads to real accomplishments and success. It's like the old nonprofit ad slogan created by the Young & Rubicam advertising agency to promote the United Negro College Fund scholarship program—a mind is a terrible thing to waste. Don't deprive the world of what you have to offer. Learn as much as you can. Learning is a lifelong, step-by-step process. Every day take at least one step toward achieving your goals. And, take pride in every step you take along the way.

Remember, an education and self-education, like everything else that's vital and valuable, doesn't come easily. But the more you learn and utilize that wisdom, the bigger payoff you'll receive, and not just financially. Knowledge also leads to placing you in those special moments, those extraordinary days that will touch you and others for the rest of your life.

To help you on this path, I've shared twenty-five years of hands-on know-how I've acquired of things to do and things not to do. A lot of it I learned the hard way. Some of it was easier, as it was shared with me or taught to me by professors, bosses, colleagues, and others. I am also grateful to everyone and everything that goads, and guides, and leads me forward. I would like to express gratitude to everyone who has been part of my life, whether professionally or personally. And to give back I have mentored a lot of people, but I want to share my knowledge with more, which is why I'm giving you the *12 Golden Keys to Hospitality Excellence*. Use them. The knowledge they impart will also give you more confidence, because when you learn how to do something you then know that you can do it, and with that comes the confidence that you will do it. And just like me, you can attain any goal you want if you focus and work hard.

For me, with this book, I'm giving you confidence, knowledge and the opportunity to change both your professional and personal life. And what of you? How do you plan to apply your knowledge of the golden keys to improve your organization and leave a lasting impact? I would like to end this book with one of my favorite quotes of all times by the late George H. W. Bush (41): "the American Dream means giving it your all, trying your hardest, accomplishing something. And then I'd add to that, giving something back. No definition of a successful life can do anything but include serving others."

Dear Reader,

I would be remiss if I didn't thank you for taking time out of your busy life to read the *12 Golden Keys to Hospitality Excellence*. I appreciate it so much, as all the hard work and long hours I put in to write this book would mean nothing if you hadn't read it. I hope you found all or some of it informative and entertaining.

With this work, I aim to offer you a practical reference guide, whether you are a current or aspiring manager in the hospitality industry, that will help you become more effective and productive while enhancing the world-class experience you deliver to your members or costumers.

I hope the hands-on knowledge I shared from cover to cover in these pages will lead you to success in your career in club management, other hospitality fields, or other industries.

I love to hear from readers as well as others in the hospitality industry. Feel free to reach out to me if you have any comments or questions on:

https://twitter.com/fhbenzakour or

www.instagram.com/fhbenzakour/

Sincerely yours,

F. H. Benzakour

Bibliography

Ho, Joan. "Creating A Hospitality Leadership Development Training Program for a Country Club" Spring 2013 https://digitalscholarship.unlv.edu/cgi/viewcontent.cgi?article=2344&context=thesesdissertations.

Kreitz, Patricia. "Best Practices for Managing Organizational Diversity." 05, 05, 2007 https://www.slac.stanford.edu/cgi-wrap/getdoc/slac-pub-12499.pdf.

McCraw, Debra. B. "5 Steps for Overcoming Diversity Challenges" 08, 15, 2017 https://www.aitp.org/blog/aitp-blog/2017/08/15/5-steps-to-overcoming-diversity-challenges/.

Updegraff, Robert Rawls. *Obvious Adams - the story of a successful businessman.* New York, NY: Harper and Brothers 09, 09, 1916.

Moeller, Eric. "Three important lessons from Obvious Adams, a business book written almost a century ago" 3, 24, 2014. http://copydojo.com/obvious-adams/.

Clem, Theresa. Ravichandran, Swathi. Kapinski, Aryn C. "Understanding country club members' loyalty: factors affecting membership renewal decisions" *Hospitality Review* Volume 31 February 2014.

Kolter, Phillip. Keller, Kevin Lane. *Marketing Management.* Upper Saddle River, NJ : Pearson Prentice Hall, 2009.

Bencito, veronica joy v. "Customer Satisfaction Among the Members of the Summit Point Golf and Country Club" *Asia Pacific Journal of Multidisciplinary Research Volume 2 April 2014.*

Walker, Callie. "15 Questions to Ask in Your Next Member Satisfaction Survey" *MC Talks The MemberClicks Blog*. 10, 15, 2018. https://blog. memberclicks.com/15-questions-to-ask-in-your-next-member-satisfaction-survey.

Reichheld, Frederick F. Sasser, Jr., W. Earl. "Zero Defections: Quality Comes to Services" *Harvard Business Review September - October 1990 Issue* https://hbr.org/1990/09/zero-defections-quality-comes-to-services

Tian-Cole, Shu. & Crompton, John. "A conceptualization of the relationships between service quality and visitor satisfaction, and their links to destination selection" *Leisure Studies 2003:* Volume 22, Issue 1, 65-80 https://www.tandfonline.com/doi/abs/10.1080/02614 360306572

Oshins, Mike. "Change in the Hospitality Industry: New Paradigms, Frames, and Perspectives" *Boston Hospitality Review* Spring 2017. http://www. bu.edu/bhr/2017/06/12/hospitality-change-paradigm-and-perspective/.

Neate, Rupert. "Dying golf clubs warned to lose the attitude and embrace young players" *The guardian.* Aug. 2016 https://www.theguardian.com/sport/2016/aug/12/golf-clubs-future-young-players-dress-code-social-media.

Grossmann, Cristian. "5 Forces of Change and How Hospitality Companies Can Adapt" *Beekeeper Blog.* https://blog.beekeeper.io/5-forces-of-change-and-how-hospitality-companies-can-adapt/.

Triumph, Krystal. "Six ways clubs can enhance service with mobile technology" *Club Management Association of America* https://www.cmaa.org/ template.aspx? id=39440.

Davies, Tikky Dawwalee. "Could game theory be your secret weapon for attracting hotel guests? *The Booking Factory.*" https://blog.thebookingfactory.com/could-game-theory-be-your-secret-weapon-for-attracting-hotel-guests-acb7b6078d9c.

"A few game theory definitions and the most applicable games" https://www.managerial-economics-club.com/game-theory-definition.html.

"Game Theory" https://www.investopedia.com/terms/g/gametheory.asp.

Spaniel, William. *Game Theory 101 the complete text book:* CreateSpace Independent Publishing Platform, 2014

Kim, W. Chan. & and Mauborgne, Renée. "Do you have the mind of a blue ocean Strategist?" *Blue Ocean Strategy.com. 4-18-2018*

https://www.blueoceanstrategy.com/blog/the-mind-of-a-blue-ocean-strategist/.

Edwards, Carlyann. "Blue Ocean Strategy: Creating Your Own Market" *Business News Daily.* 7 -13-2018 https://www.businessnewsdaily.com/5647-blue-ocean-strategy.html

Anastasia. "Strategic Framework: Understanding Blue Ocean Strategy" *Cleverism.* 7 – 16 -2015. https://www.cleverism.com/understanding-blue-ocean-strategy-strategic-framework/.

Kruse, Kevin. "The 80/20 Rule And How It Can Change Your Life" forbes.com. *03-07-2016.* https://www.forbes.com/sites/kevinkruse/2016/03/07/80-20-rule/#3fc753df3814.

Abrams, Jackie. *Social Media for Private Clubs: Platforms & Privacy, NationalClub.org/news, 0* 8- 01-2013

Erind, Bella, *Companies that blog have 434% more indexed pages. And companies with more indexed pages get far more leads, LinkedIn .com /pulse,* October 9, 2014

Quote from George Bush. *"Patriarch of a Political Dynasty". The Academy of Achievement Interview in Williamsburg, Virginia, www.achievement.org. June 2, 1995.*